GUNDOGS

GUNDOGS

Their Care and Training

SECOND EDITION

MICHAEL BRANDER

ADAM & CHARLES BLACK
LONDON

SECOND EDITION 1983
FIRST PUBLISHED 1963
REPRINTED 1969, 1972 AND 1976
A. & C. BLACK (PUBLISHERS) LTD.
35 BEDFORD ROW, LONDON WC1R 4JH

ISBN 0 7136 2309 8

Brander, Michael
Gundogs. — 2nd ed.
1. Hunting dogs 2. Dogs — Training
I. Title
636.7'52 SF428.5
ISBN 0-7136-2309-8

Printed in Great Britain

PREFACE

This is a general-purpose book on gundog training. As such I have attempted to cover briefly as much ground as possible from the viewpoint of the absolute beginner. Hints are included on subjects ranging from the initial choice of a gundog through to the care of a whelping bitch, as well as suggestions on training, and in this revised edition a chapter on working tests and field trials has been added, but the book is not intended as an encyclopaedic and infallible manual of instruction. There is a great deal about gundogs, or indeed any animals, which can never be learned from any book. Something may be gained from the experience of others, but the best teachers are undoubtedly the animals themselves.

Each dog is, and should be regarded by his handler as, an individual, as different from the next as one human being from another. Thus, though certain methods of training may be suggested and occasionally alternatives indicated as well, these are purely for the handler's guidance. It is essential that he should know in his own mind what he is trying to achieve before he starts training his dog, but there should be no attempt to apply a rigid training schedule. He should appreciate that training methods must be kept elastic, since their application may well vary with each dog, although certain basic principles remain the same. The handler will do well to forget any preconceived ideas he may have formed and simply let the dog act as his guide as to what methods to use.

Even the experienced handler should always be prepared to learn from his dog, and a good gundog full of instinct can go more than half-way towards training an inexperienced handler if the latter is prepared to learn from him. Working in conjunction, they can eventually achieve a partnership in which each assists the other to the best of his ability. It is in the attainment of this harmony and understanding that the real satisfaction of gundog training lies.

1983

CONTENTS

LIST OF ILLUSTRATIONS

CHAPTER ONE

PRIOR TO TRAINING

DURING THE TRAINING of a gundog a bond of great strength should be formed between handler and dog. It is therefore desirable that gundog owners should train their own dogs if possible. Many people are probably chary of doing so, because they imagine, quite wrongly, that it is a difficult business requiring considerable time, expense and experience. While experience can be useful, as in anything else, in practice it is not essential. Nor should any expensive equipment be required. All that is really necessary is a length of strong cord, a blank pistol, some easily made dummies and an occasional assistant. A small field, or paddock, for the initial lessons, where a degree of privacy can be assured, is also desirable, but almost any open space will do as long as the pup is not distracted by outside influences. The earliest lessons of all can take place inside the house in any large room.

Granted that these facilities are available and that a regular period can be set aside each day, even if only half an hour, then the handler is ready to start. It is essential, of course, as has been noted in the Preface already, that he should be absolutely clear in his own mind what he wants his dog to do. One certain cause of failure in gundog training is any confusion in the handler's mind.

Clearly if the handler is uncertain what he wishes the dog to do he cannot expect the dog to make up his mind for him and somehow mysteriously divine his wishes. Yet there are those unreasonable enough to expect the dog to do just that, or so it would sometimes appear from their behaviour. Others seem to expect machine-like responses to whistles and commands which have not first been properly taught.

There are people who simply do not seem able to grasp that a dog's mind works differently from the human mind. They even fail to appreciate that unless commands are first properly taught shouting them loudly will have no effect whatsoever. The same mentality imagines that all foreigners must understand English if it is bellowed loudly enough. Such people apparently cannot understand that a dog's actions are largely governed by instinct and by association of ideas in the dog's mind. The handler must therefore attempt to utilize the instinct and build up gradually a series of associations in the dog's mind which they both understand.

That the association of ideas formed in the dog's mind may be entirely different from what the handler fondly imagines is one of the pitfalls of training. A common example frequently seen is when the handler puts on the lead and takes the pup out for a walk. An open space is reached and the lead is removed. The pup has a fine romp. His name is called and when he comes the lead is put on and he is taken home. Naturally he associates in his mind being called and put on the lead with the curtailment of his freedom. Next time he thinks twice about coming. A resistance is gradually building up in his mind, whereas a little thought would soon show that it is advisable to call the pup at intervals during his time off the lead. When he comes he should be rewarded and sometimes the lead put on for a few minutes before he is allowed off once more. The association in his mind will then be with a possible reward for coming in answer to his name, not with returning home, or curtailment of his freedom, which he regards in the light of a punishment.

Lack of ability to understand the dog's mind, or the dog's reactions, in this way is responsible for a great deal of the trouble people have in dog training. To help him understand his pup's mind the handler should study the way the pup conveys his feelings. A wag of the tail will indicate pleasure, the ears laid back possibly fear or obstinacy, the ears cocked forward an effort at understanding. Each dog has his own unconscious methods of signalling his reactions and it is up to the handler to learn them early and watch them constantly.

I am sure that as well as this inability to understand the dog's feelings much of the trouble people have is also due to an inability to communicate their own feelings wholeheartedly to their dogs. They can readily enough show their displeasure, but they do not take equal trouble to see that the pup is also aware of their pleasure. A faint and half-hearted 'Good dog' simply is not enough. At any rate in the early stages the pup should be patted, fondled, caressed and made much of verbally with frequent 'Good dog', 'Good boy' and similar verbal encouragement. Clear two-way communication and understanding between dog and handler is the essential basis of all training and it must be built up from small beginnings such as these.

Verbal encouragement must, however, not be confused with softness and lack of purpose. Once training has begun and an order has been heard and clearly understood no failure to obey first time should be overlooked. Every fault should be noticed and checked, if only verbally, and at the same time every act of good behaviour should be praised, or rewarded. The handler should never give an order without seeing that it is properly obeyed if possible, and he should always try, at least in the early stages of training, to put himself in a position to ensure instant obedience without resort to punishment. It is vitally important that orders should be obeyed immediately during training, for slackness in this respect, or nagging repetition, invariably leads to disobedience.

If any faults are overlooked during training, they are naturally infinitely harder to overcome later when they have become ingrained, but carelessness, or slackness, on the handler's part at any time will soon be sensed by the dog and reflected in his disobedient behaviour. Even a fully trained dog can very quickly learn bad habits, and the old saying 'Months to make and moments to spoil', like most old saws, has its kernel of truth. For this reason as much as any other the sound professional trainer will not consider his work complete until he sees the dog he has trained and the owner he has trained him for working together.

The man who buys a trained dog must appreciate that he is in effect paying for the work the trainer has put into the dog over the previous months or even years as well as for the dog itself. To my mind this is not a thing that can be assessed adequately in terms of money or necessarily even bought. The new owner may buy the dog, but he cannot buy instant obedience from the dog, nor should he expect to do so. He has not bought a machine and cannot expect machine-like responses. It is up to him to take over from where the trainer has left off. He may have come to terms with the trainer, but he still has to come to terms with the dog.

There are some people who through harshness or impatience or merely lack of understanding will inevitably spoil any dog, however well trained, and then the professional's work has been wasted. Fortunately understanding and sympathy with the canine mind, that quality of natural understanding and sympathy which with horses has its equivalent in someone with natural 'hands', is not so uncommon. It must not, however, be confused with sentimental love and affection. Doting affection is usually allied to complete lack of real understanding and can lead to more harmful handling than results from loss of temper and impatience. Either is likely to lead to a complete failure in training.

Another reason for failure to train a gundog successfully may lie with the dog itself. It may seem unnecessary to point out that by the very nature of things all gundogs should be bred for use with the gun, but this is unfortunately by no means always the case. Although shows and field trials were originally introduced to improve the looks and performance of working gundogs, they have long since become an end in themselves. Show-bench strains and field-trial strains of the same breeds of gundog frequently bear little relationship to each other or to genuine working strains. There are, regrettably enough, some field-trial strains which are not worked with the gun at all, or alternatively so selectively as to mean next to nothing. As is well known, many show strains have long passed the stage where the gun means anything to them at all. If the beginner is unfortunate enough to start with a dog of such breeding, where the instinct is no longer dominant, he is handicapping himself at once.

It is also important that the beginner should choose the type of dog most suited for the sort of shooting he enjoys, but when it comes to making a choice he is likely to find himself encountering a surprising barrier of prejudice and myth erected by the supporters and opponents of the various gundog breeds. Whatever their bias, whether it is 'Show' versus 'Trials', 'Black Labrador' versus 'Yellow Labrador', 'Specialist' versus 'Spaniel or Pointer-Retriever', or just 'English' versus 'Foreign', dog-owners can be surprisingly partisan and bitter in spite of the fact that a gundog owner should be first and foremost a sportsman. It is up to the beginner to decide for himself whether in practice these divisions and barriers between the breeds and subdivisions of breeds amount to anything of real substance or whether they are merely founded on blind prejudice and ignorance.

It is worth just briefly examining the background. Before the Kennel Club was formed in 1873 and began to register the breeding of dogs systematically, most gundogs were, to put it mildly, somewhat haphazardly bred. There were few accurate breeding records and even the recognized breeds were not long stabilized from their original crosses. To take only two instances the English Pointer was originally produced by crosses with the old Spanish Pointer and the English foxhound. The Labrador Retriever was originally bred from Newfoundland crosses. Quite a number of the breeds we know today did not exist and those that did are now greatly changed.

At that time also the roles of the various gundogs were far from settled. Prior to the development of the breech-loader, Pointers and Setters were generally expected to retrieve and face cover or water. The Gordon Setter was indeed famed as a general-purpose dog in Germany before the German Shorthaired Pointer was developed there in the 1870's as a recognized breed with crosses of English and Spanish Pointer. In short, if you go back far enough there is little to pick and choose between the various breeds. None of which alters the fact that a good gundog working well in its chosen role is a joy to watch and a prejudiced owner is a bore in any language.

The Kennel Club, by exercising supervision and control, has produced order out of chaos and now lists four categories of gundogs. They are firstly *Retrievers*, which includes Black or Yellow Labradors, Golden Retrievers, Chesapeakes, and Flat or Curly Coated Retrievers. Secondly there are *Pointers and Setters*, which includes English Pointers and English, Irish, and Gordon Setters. Thirdly there are *Spaniels*, which includes English or Welsh Springers, Clumbers, Cockers, Sussex and Irish Water Spaniels. Fourthly there are *German Shorthaired Pointers and those breeds which hunt, point, and retrieve*. This includes Weimaraners and Magyar Vyszlas, i.e. Hungarian Pointers. The Large and Small Munsterlanders, wire-haired Pointers and other pointer-retriever breeds should also be included.

It must be left to the individual to make his own inquiries about each breed and form his own decisions about which will suit him and his particular requirements best. For the man living on a wildfowling estuary a Cocker Spaniel may be obviously the wrong choice as being unequal to retrieving a wounded goose. For the man living in a town a German Shorthaired Pointer may be equally wrong, as are likely to be any of the larger gundog breeds. An overweight and under-exercised gundog wheezing asthmatically after his master amid the diesel fumes of any busy town pavement is always a pathetic spectacle. Yet there are exceptions even to such broad generalizations, and it must be left to each individual after he has made due inquiry to make his own choice for himself. If he rushes to buy the first dog he sees of the first breed which catches his attention, then he deserves all he gets. It is only unfortunate that the dog must suffer for his mistakes.

Breeding any animal successfully is a skilled business, where background knowledge of blood lines and different strains can result in a steady improvement in type and performance. This should be the aim and object of any serious breeder of animals. The Kennel Club lays down the recognized breed standards for each breed within which limits they are supposed to conform and one would suppose that this was enough. Unfortunately, as has already been pointed out, there are owners and breeders whose aim is limited solely to success in shows or field trials, and steady breeding for such ends has led to sometimes quite amazing deviations in type and performance between dogs of the same breed, quite without reference to these Kennel Club standards. This is, to say the least, a shortsighted policy.

Unfortunately there is also a great deal of what is best termed 'haphazard' breeding of dogs. It is astounding how ignorant many dog-owners are and how blind they can be to obvious defects in their dogs. It is common enough to meet owners who do not know the points of a dog and that, I suppose, may be excused, but I have met owners, and this is no exaggeration, who did not even know what breed of dog it was they owned. In the face of such astonishing ignorance such matters as blood lines and breed standards are on a different plane.

Yet, either because they hope to make a little easy money, or because they feel it is the thing to do and good for the bitch, such people are generally ready enough to breed, although they have only the barest idea of what is involved. Too often one hears of a casual breeder who discovered after the mating that the next-door dog he used as a sire was the litter brother of his bitch. That both may be descended from a line known to have hysteria, hip dysplasia, crypt-orchidism, or some equally serious hereditary fault is almost certainly outside his ken, but it is not likely in any case to deter him from trying to sell his pups if the bitch manages to raise them without accident. Nor, from motives of mistaken humanity or for purely mercenary reasons, is such an inexperienced breeder likely to cull the indifferent puppies from the litter.

Enough has been said, I hope, to make the beginner cautious in his approach to buying a pup. Having made certain in his own mind which breed he prefers, he cannot do better than approach the Kennel Club, or the Breed Club Secretary, for the names of some reputable breeders of working gundogs who may have pups available. A well-known breeder has his reputation to consider, and although his pups may cost more initially, they are likely to prove far cheaper in the long run, for there is nothing more expensive than a useless dog, however cheap it was to buy.

It is advisable to see both the sire and the dam of the litter if this is possible and learn something of their background breeding, their achievements, if any, and their working ability. For the protection of both parties it is a sound principle to insist on a veterinary certificate, and any breeder who is not prepared to provide this is best left severely alone. A reputable breeder will generally insist on this himself and will be only too pleased to tell the prospective purchaser anything he cares to know. If he is given reasonable warning, he will usually be prepared to demonstrate his dogs in action. After all this, it merely remains to choose a pup.

When it comes to the actual choice of a pup from a litter it is always difficult to give any sound advice. It is advisable to check the jaws for bite. They should be neither overshot nor undershot, but should meet cleanly. It is also advisable to check the eyes for defective vision and ingrowing eyelids. In the case of a dog pup it is as well to make sure that both testicles have dropped. Otherwise it is only possible to advocate choosing a pup with no obvious deformities and with as much bone as possible. It is not like buying a horse, when a good shoulder, quality and general conformation tend to show clearly enough in a foal in spite of its general legginess.

No one can be certain of always picking the best pup from a litter at weaning stage. Most breeders will admit it can sometimes happen that the ugliest pup turns out to be the best when they are fully grown. By watching the pups' behaviour intently it may be possible to form some idea of their various temperaments and this is probably as good a guide as any if there is little else to pick and choose between them. An alert quick pup is probably a good choice, but this may be very misleading. As the pup develops so its temperament is liable to alter, although, of course, environment and training have a great deal to do with this. There is no doubt however that seeing the sire and dam beforehand can be a great help in choosing a pup, as then it is possible to form some idea of how the pups are likely to develop later.

As a matter of course, it is worth clapping the hands loudly together in the presence of the pups to see how they react. If the pups do not object to this, the chances are that they will not later on object to the gun. In practice real cases of gunshyness in gundogs bred for the gun are probably much rarer than is imagined. Gun nervousness, caused by careless introduction to the gun, which is generally curable, is another matter, and very much more common, being frequently mistaken for the former. In any event clapping the hands is likely to give the prospective owner a chance to assess the pup's general reactions and some idea of whether it is forward and bold, or shy and retiring.

Once the breed and the pup have been chosen the question arises whether or not he should live in the house. There is little doubt that, strictly speaking, a gundog ought to live in a kennel, since in the house he is inevitably subject to distracting influences. Kept in a kennel he is likely to await his daily exercise and lessons with keenness and enthusiasm. Yet many one-dog owners will probably prefer to keep the dog in the house if possible. A great deal, of course, must depend on the dog and the household. If the members of the household all understand at least the elements of gundog training and can be relied on not to spoil the pup, the results may be most satisfactory. If the pup pines in the solitary confinement of a kennel, it may in any case be preferable to have him in the house, but then the household must first be 'trained'.

If the pup is kept in the house, the stresses and strains of modern living are such that it is clearly essential to have some safety factors. He must have his own basket, or private corner of his own, free from draughts and distractions, to which he can retire. As far as possible, within reason, he should be allowed peace and quiet.

At the same time, whether kept in the house or a kennel, he should gradually be accustomed to journeys in the car and to meeting new people and visiting fresh places. In this way he will very quickly have a considerable advantage over the pup which remains permanently in his kennel and rarely goes outside. Such a pup will probably be terrified by his first experiences of modern traffic and crowds. Nor will he have the same opportunities for developing his intelligence.

I have heard it argued that intelligence is not always required in a gundog and that instinct is more desirable. Admittedly instinct strongly developed is a most desirable trait in any gundog, but intelligence is also highly desirable and it can be enhanced both by training and environment. Intelligent co-operation is an asset in any gundog. An intelligent dog readily responding to his handler's commands is a delight to own.

It must be remembered that although dogs do not

think in the same way as humans they differ quite as much as humans both in intelligence and ability. Almost inevitably some will develop faster than others. It is, for instance, usual for bitches to be considerably quicker and readier to learn than dogs. Some pups, like some humans, will be slow to learn, but once they have grasped a lesson will not forget it. Others will be quick to learn and just as quick to forget. Yet others will be very quick to learn and very easily bored if a lesson is too prolonged.

From this it will be appreciated that no one can do more than generalize on the subject of when training should begin and how and at what speed or in what order it should continue. So much must be dependent on the pup and on his handler. One man may know instinctively what to do and achieve wonders with an indifferent pup. Another may achieve similar results, but only because his pup was crammed full of instinct, so that it was almost impossible for him to go wrong.

The easiest pitfall of all for the keen beginner is to try to start training his pup too intensively at too early an age. Most pups are not mature enough for intensive training until they are from six to nine months old. At the same time no harm may be done in starting a certain limited preliminary training from the moment the pup is weaned, although it is most important never to overdo it. If the pup is being overtrained or forced along too fast in this way he will probably begin to make obvious mistakes and refuse to obey commands. He will also usually begin to show lack of interest and loss of enthusiasm for his lessons. The only effective remedy then is for the handler to abandon training completely for a while until the pup recovers his keenness and zest once more. It is to be hoped that thereafter the handler will have learned his lesson and continue only at the pup's pace.

Throughout the training the handler should always study the pup in this way. He must try always to be one jump ahead and anticipate the pup's likely reactions in any situation. It is essential at all stages to maintain the pup's interest. At any sign of boredom it is advisable to stop training for the moment. It is in any case always better to have several short training sessions rather than one long one with the accompanying risk of boredom.

It is a temptation to the keen beginner to prolong a lesson in an effort to make his pup perform it really well. Although it is always important to try to end a lesson successfully, it is often better to stop in the middle rather than force an issue and risk being defeated. If there is any danger of this, it is far better to change over to some simple command, which will be readily obeyed, and, after duly rewarding the pup with a pat, end the lesson on a good note. Next time the more difficult lesson can be taken up again and the chances are it will be performed correctly.

Most gundog training is simply a matter of channelling the natural instincts of the dog into the required paths. Punishment, if it is administered at all, must be coincidental with the offence, but if possible it is far better to avoid giving the dog the chance to commit the offence in the first place. The handler should always be thinking ahead, like the driver of a car with his eye on the road in front, prepared to avoid trouble before it arises.

The beginner must appreciate that all will not always go well. He must expect setbacks of a temporary nature occasionally. Sometimes they may even appear to be extremely serious, but it is as well not to be too easily depressed. He or his pup may have been off colour for a day or two. There may have been undue stress on some aspect of the training, or insufficient time spent on another point. A change of subject or a temporary holiday when things seem to be going wrong can often work wonders. It is as well never to try to hurry things in dog training. It is also important to bear in mind that the object is to train the dog to work with the gun and not to allow the lessons to become an end in themselves.

Once the work in the field starts it should only be considered that the handler and the dog have begun their advanced training together. From that stage on it should become increasingly a partnership in which each plays an active part and in which each relies to some extent on the other. Each should be prepared to learn from the other. In their partnership and reliance on each other should be a great part of the enjoyment of their sport.

CHAPTER TWO

INITIAL TRAINING

ONCE THE MOST SUITABLE BREED has been decided on and a pup finally chosen the earliest stages should consist, as has been noted, in studying the pup and gaining his confidence fully. Although there should be no hurry about any stage, at the same time it is as well for the handler to start as he means to go on. A pup taken from a litter where he has had the company of his litter brothers and sisters is inevitably going to feel lonely and miserable when he is first left by himself. He will almost certainly howl his misery to the skies and take some considerable time to settle down in his new surroundings. If the new owner is foolish enough to take any notice of this disturbance, then the pup has at once established a precedent and has won the first round. In effect the pup has trained his handler to accept that when the pup howls the handler must come. If no one comes the pup will eventually realize that howling is a waste of time. This may sound heartless, but it is sense.

None of the foregoing means to imply that the utmost care should not be taken to make the pup comfortable and to make him feel at home and interested in his new surroundings. If he is given a straw bed in a new kennel a very good way of accustoming him to his new surroundings is to rub straw from his bed over his body and behind his ears so that it carries the scent of his body on it. He will thus not feel that he is in strange surroundings and will tend to snuggle down amidst the familiar odour of his own body scent. The same principle will hold good with his blankets in his basket if he is given a basket in the house. A warm drink of milk, with possibly a little aspirin in it, last thing before he is left, making sure that he has a run on grass immediately afterwards to give him a chance to empty his bladder before he beds down, then he should be left severely alone, however much he may howl. In practice if the foregoing precautions have all been taken and the pup has had a tiring day, as he probably will have had with the emotional disturbance of a change of home, he will more than likely soon retire to bed and to sleep.

The customary kennel routine of a run last thing at night and first thing in the morning should be adhered to from the start. At first the pup should also be given a run immediately before and after any meal as well as after any excitement. If at any time the pup is caught on the point of fouling the house, he should at once be taken outside and encouraged to continue there. If he fouls the house unnoticed, disapproval should be shown and the pup again put outside.

When the pup is kept in the house his house-training may be a fair indication of how his future training will go, but no more. Some dogs are naturally clean and will never foul their kennels, or the house, and others are natural born sluts. The latter may be full of instinct and may make excellent gundogs, so that if there is trouble in house-training do not despair. At the same time, if the pup is always put out as suggested, the message should soon go home, or perhaps it would be more to the point to say that eventually the penny will drop.

It must be appreciated that this sort of thing may take longer with some dogs than with others and there are always admittedly exceptions to every rule. Yet at the same time this is one of the first and most elementary points of training, and it should be noted that it can be successfully achieved simply by regularity without the pup even realizing that anything is being taught. The preliminary obedience training on which all the more advanced training is based can almost all be taught in a similarly easy way by regular repetition of simple commands or signals.

An important point that must always be borne in mind is that all commands used should be short, clear and with no resemblance to each other. It does not in the least matter what words of command are used as long as these points are observed, and as long as the same command is always used in the same way, so that no confusion can be caused in the pup's mind as to what is meant. Confused commands or verbose commands such as: 'Hi, you, dog. Come on over here, you brute!' when the command 'Heel' prefaced by the dog's name would have been enough is the sort of thing which only leads to trouble.

In this connexion it is as well to choose a name for the dog which is not easily confused with any of the commands to be used. Like the commands, however, it should be short. One or two syllables is enough for a working name. To begin with at least it should always be used before each command to attract the pup's attention in the same way that all commands in the Services are prefaced with a warning 'Squad' or group title. Later on a warning whistle to attract the pup's attention and prepare it for the command or signal may be enough, but the principle remains the same.

It is also extremely important to remember that the early commands should always be given in the same tone of voice. Perhaps tone by itself is a misleading description. A voice over the telephone may be pitched in a tone devoid of any feeling, so that while the message may come over there is no life in it. When addressing the pup the handler's tone should be full of life, inspiring the pup. It is difficult to stress sufficiently to the beginner how important this question of tone can be.

A good example of the same thing is encountered when exercising a young horse on a lunge line. Control then is virtually entirely by voice, and the horse's pace can be altered merely by the tone of voice repeating the required commands. Thus 'Walk' becomes a cautionary 'Wau-au-alk', 'Trot' becomes a crisp 'Ter-rot', and 'Canter' becomes an almost sing-song 'Can-tah'. In the same way the commands to the pup will undergo a natural alteration differing with each handler, but the important point is that they should always be clear, distinct, full of life, and with the same intonation.

In the early stages especially a sensitive pup can easily be overawed and frightened by the human voice raised in angry tones, or by the accusing human eye. It is important in the early stages to keep the tone of voice cheerful and encouraging, whatever one's inner feelings may be. It should hardly be necessary to add that especially with young pups it is most important never to lose either patience or temper. If there is any danger of that, the lesson should be stopped at once and continued later.

The question of whether to give any biscuit, or titbit, when the pup has performed correctly can be a difficult one. To start with it may well be advisable to encourage the pup with a piece of biscuit or similar titbit, as the best way to a pup's affections is frequently through his stomach. In the early stages, especially when teaching him to come, a biscuit may prove a useful bribe. Later on an occasional biscuit may be given as a reward for especially good work, but a pup which is always looking for a piece of biscuit can be a nuisance, and it may well tend to distract his attention from the lesson. Although there are undoubtedly times when it can be useful, it is advisable to avoid indiscriminate rewards of this nature.

The first command which it is probably necessary to teach, as it is used in connexion with the training outlined above, is the general prohibition 'No'. A pup about to foul the house is restrained with the command 'No', before being put outside. A wildly enthusiastic pup jumping up in a bumbling fashion may be restrained and gently but firmly put down, with the admonition 'No'. The pup will soon appreciate that this is a general prohibition against transgression of one sort or another. Its use, however, should not be overdone in the early stages and it should only be used when the order can, if necessary, be sharply reinforced to point the lesson. Great care must always be exercised not to sicken a sensitive pup by excessive nagging use of this command.

Coincidental with this the command 'Kennel', or 'Basket', should also be learned. This should be repeated in firm, but not loud, tones while the pup is placed in the position required. If he attempts to come out the command should be repeated, together with the prohibition 'No', and the pup replaced gently but firmly in the kennel or basket. He may then be made much of, but first the command must have been properly obeyed. A very few repetitions of this will probably be sufficient and the pup should soon appreciate the meaning of the command.

It should scarcely need to be stressed that no matter what the provocation, and admittedly pups can sometimes unwittingly be very provoking, the handler should never lose his temper with a pup. If he feels at any time that there is a danger of him doing so, he should at once return the pup to his kennel and himself retire until he can continue the lesson in a calmer frame of mind. Loss of temper will almost certainly result in loss of the pup's confidence in his handler.

It might also be pointed out that, although a mature dog may be a different matter, a young pup should never be beaten. If it is felt necessary to punish a pup at any time, the best method of doing so is by shaking him. Hold him firmly by the loose skin on either side of the neck and give him a good shaking. This will be as effective as any beating. The pup may also be effectively punished by verbal admonition in disgusted tones.

Unless cause and effect are clearly associated in the pup's mind, any form of punishment is better left until an opportunity arises again, when it should be applied at once. Here again is one of the pitfalls of training. What may seem to be clearly associated in the handler's mind may not be associated at all in the pup's mind. For instance, a pup runs after a hen outside a poultry run. On his return the handler scolds him. Naturally the pup associates the scolding with his return, not with chasing the hen. Next time he may be chary of returning. In such an instance it would be far better to give him another chance to chase and check him in time with a severe rating.

Constant resort to punishment of any sort is an admission of failure, but at the same time transgression should never be allowed to pass unchecked. Prompt checking in time is worth any amount of punishment after the event. Intelligent anticipation of the pup's actions and immediate verbal checking beforehand whenever he is in two minds about committing an offence will in most cases avoid the need for any more drastic action.

CHAPTER THREE

BASIC PRELIMINARY TRAINING

THE INITIAL INTRODUCTORY TRAINING has taught the pup the meaning of the command 'No' and of 'Kennel' or 'Basket'. He has also begun to respond to his name. Once these very elementary commands have been properly learned and the pup has gained complete confidence in his handler it is time, to my mind, to continue with the basic preliminary training. The aim of this is to teach the pup to walk at heel, to come to heel from a distance at command, signal or whistle, to drop at command, signal or whistle, also later shot, both near at hand and at a distance, and finally to stay put at command or signal. This may well seem at first sight as if it is forcing too much on the pup all at once, and it must be stressed that this is not an immediate process but a gradual one. It must also be realized that this is all covered by the two commands 'Heel' and 'Sit' and by the signals of a hand patted against the knee or thigh for 'Heel' and a raised hand or stamped foot for 'Sit'.

It will be appreciated that all this does not mean to say that the pup should not be encouraged to play in the normal puppy way. In fact, I am in favour of providing the pup with some toys to keep him occupied. Apart from any other considerations, this is likely to stop him from becoming bored and from chewing his kennel or his basket as a diversion. It may also help to teach him retrieving later. As far as possible, however, a clear-cut distinction should be drawn between play and any lesson which is being taught, although it is equally desirable that the pup should enjoy his lessons as far as is compatible with discipline.

Although the outline of the basic preliminary training given above may seem a great deal to a human being, it should be realized that the process of teaching is such a gradual one that it can, in fact, be easily absorbed by the average pup. The important point once the pup's confidence has been gained is to establish a routine, since regularity as well as repetition will help to imprint the lessons more readily in the pup's mind, although regularity and routine must never be allowed to degenerate into boredom.

During this training especially it must be borne in mind that the human figure towers over a pup and the human voice, unless pitched in encouraging tones, can easily sound very formidable to a young animal. Remembering this, it will be appreciated that the raised hand may easily be interpreted wrongly by a sensitive pup as a threatening gesture, just as the raised voice may be interpreted as a warning of punishment to come. Failure to look at matters from the pup's viewpoint in this way may easily lead to apparent disobedience, when, in fact, it is the handler who is at fault. As a general rule the blame for any disobedience on the pup's part can be laid squarely on the handler's shoulders, for it is he who is to blame for allowing the situation to get out of control.

In the very earliest stages this basic training may start with the handler going to the pup's basket, or kennel, putting on his collar and lead, and leading the pup, at heel in the position he will later be expected to adopt, to the centre of the room, or kennel run. The command 'Heel' should be repeated to impress the point on the pup if he does not maintain his correct position and attempts to stray, as he very probably will do, and at the same time he should be firmly returned to the correct

Early retrieving with twelve week old puppy: squatting to encourage a fearless return.

Using a wall to teach the youngster to maintain the correct heel position.

position. On halting, the command 'Sit' should be given and the pup gently but firmly pushed into a sitting position. This may well be enough for the very earliest lesson.

The extension of this lesson is simply that, having halted with the pup at heel, the handler turns round, still holding the lead, and faces the pup. Holding his hand above his head palm outwards in the universal halt sign, he should then take a step backwards, repeating the command 'Sit'. It is probable the pup will try to move, whereupon a warning, firm 'No' should be given and the command 'Sit' repeated. If the pup has moved, he should be gently pushed back into the position he has left and the command again repeated. This may well be enough in the first instance.

Meanwhile whenever the pup is being fed the command 'Sit' may also be used. As the pup will almost certainly sit if the food dish is held above him, this is usually very easily effected. If he does not sit at once, the command should be gently enforced by pushing him into the required position, at the same time repeating the command. Once again by repetition the command will probably be very quickly associated with the action, and as the reward will seem very considerable the pup is likely to respond very readily to it.

The obvious extension of this is to keep him sitting when the food is placed in front of him. Along with the command 'Sit' a hand may be raised above the head and a foot stamped, if these signals are both going to be used. The pup should then be restrained for a moment or two when the food is placed in front of him, until the command 'Right' or a click of the fingers is given with a reassuring pat. This is akin to the 'On Trust' trick which most pet dogs learn and apart from anything else it is good obedience training. Care should, however, be exercised with a fussy eater to avoid undue use of the command 'No' if possible, as this may be inclined to give the pup inhibitions and make him even faddier about eating.

Taking this a stage further, the next step is to make the pup sit while placing the food dish some feet away from him. Should he try to move forward, he must be gently but firmly placed back in the identical position he left. After holding this position for a few moments the food dish may be placed in front of him and he may be encouraged to eat with the command 'Right'. Gradually the distance the pup is made to sit from the food dish and the length of time elapsing before he is allowed to eat may be increased. In the early stages, at least, it is advisable that the food dish should be taken to the pup rather than that he be allowed to go to it. The point it is desired to associate in the pup's mind with reward is sitting still to command; therefore at all times any attempt to move must be firmly checked and the pup at once replaced in the position he has left.

To enforce the point of this training really effectively a check cord can be useful. This is merely a length of strong cord attached to the pup's collar. If it is desired to stop the pup going away from the handler, it can be left trailing free within easy reach. If it is desired to stop the pup coming towards the handler, it can be led round a fence pole, or a tree, if out of doors, or through the kennel fencing if in the kennel run, or round any convenient heavy piece of furniture if indoors. The direction of pull on the pup will then be away from the handler. Should the pup start running towards the handler and fail to check at once when the command 'Sit' is given, or at the sight of a raised hand, then a jerk on the check cord will bring him up sharply. He should then be replaced in the position he has left and the lesson will not have to be repeated often.

While aiming at repetition and routine to impress the lessons on the pup's mind the handler should also strive for variety to avoid boredom. As an example he may go to the basket or kennel in the early stages and put on the collar and lead with the check cord attached. He may then walk back several paces, reiterating the command 'Basket' or 'Kennel', if the pup should try to follow him. Then, still holding the check lead, he may turn round away from the pup and with the gesture of patting his knee, or thigh, call the pup to heel with the command 'Heel', preceded by the pup's name. Should the pup show any signs of straying the check cord may be used, but it is unlikely that it will be necessary if the pup's keenness has been properly maintained. This is incidentally one of the occasions when a piece of biscuit may not be amiss as a reward, and in any case on coming to heel correctly the pup should certainly be made much of in the early stages. It is also important to remember that a sensitive pup may easily be deterred by the effect of the handler's gaze. It is as well to keep the head and eyes averted during this and the early retrieving lessons.

Each day the object should be to vary the pattern of the lessons, thus maintaining the pup's interest constantly while slowly increasing the number and scope of the commands to which he responds. Thus when he answers readily to the command 'Heel' and the signal of the hand patting the knee, or thigh, the command may be dropped and the signal alone used. From that it is a small but logical and easy step for him to answer the signal and the recall whistle. Soon he should respond freely to any one or any combinations of these. In order to maintain his interest the changes should be rung from time to time and no mistakes should be overlooked.

If the pup is trained to obey the command 'Sit' in conjunction with the food training and the check cord,

Encouraging a twelve week old pup to sit when halted in the early stages of lead training.

as has been suggested, the signals or the raised hand and stamped foot recommended will soon be firmly associated with the command in the pup's mind. Either of the signals or the command should be sufficient to cause the pup to drop at once. Furthermore the handler should appreciate that the command as well as meaning 'Sit' in the pup's mind also means 'Stay'. The pup should never be allowed to move from the drop without a further command from the handler. In the earliest stages, as has already been noted, it is advisable always to go up to the pup before giving him any further command once he has been dropped at a distance. He should then be rewarded for sitting still before the next command is given, and in this way he will soon become thoroughly steady and reliable at the drop, remaining unmoving once he has been given the command or signal.

In practice, with careful advances of a little more each day it should soon be possible for the handler to walk away from the pup sitting at the drop, after the command or signals, and even go out of sight, secure in the knowledge that the pup will not move, nor, if his food is present, touch it without permission. Of course the steps towards this must be carefully assessed as within the pup's powers. Starting with the check cord and one or two paces taken away from the pup, the progress thereafter must depend on the pup's ability. In the first instances it is naturally desirable to choose a position where though out of sight of the pup he can still be kept in view and checked by command if necessary.

When the pup is really steady and reliable at the drop the training may be varied considerably. On being called to heel from a distance the pup may readily be checked on the way and dropped by command or signal while still some way away from the handler. It is naturally a simple step once the signals are firmly associated with the command in the pup's mind to substitute the drop whistle for the command. Thereafter the signals, the command, and the whistle may be alternated to keep the pup's interest. Once again, however, mistakes must not be overlooked.

The type of whistle used does not really matter. It may be a two-tone whistle, or a so-called 'silent' whistle, or any other preferred. The pup could if desired be trained to respond to a hunting horn or a bugle. It might, however, just be noted that a beginner using a 'silent' whistle would be advised to use it at full volume, so that he can be sure his pup hears it. Otherwise he himself may be uncertain that the pup has done so, and this uncertainty can lead to repetition or inconsistency and hence to disobedience. Consistency is vital, whatever signals are used.

It may be that a series of blasts are meant to represent 'Heel' and a single long blast 'Sit', as is probably the most common, but it could be the reverse. By the method indicated the pup can gradually be taught whatever private language the handler cares to use to convey his meaning to him. As long as the whistle is always used in the same way to mean the same thing and the command is promptly obeyed, nothing else matters.

In the same way with the signals and commands, it does not in the least matter what they are as long as they are consistent. The pup could as easily be taught to sit to the command 'Stand' or to come to the raised hand. I have suggested the more obvious commands which do not easily conflict with each other and which are easily remembered by the handler. It might at this point be noted that to have two signals for the drop may at times be found useful. There are times when it is not possible, or desirable, to raise the hand, and the stamped foot can be seen and recognized at a surprising distance: so, it may be added, can the hand patting the thigh or knee for the recall to heel.

Carrying on from this stage, the pup may be tried out with the blank pistol. Assuming that he has no objection to loudly clapped hands, it is unlikely that he will be frightened by the blank pistol, but in any case the first shot should be fired behind the handler's back in the open at some distance from the pup, so that the handler can observe the effect. In all probability the pup will merely look round inquiringly for the source of the unexpected noise. Thereafter the next shot may be fired in the air with the hand raised as for the signal to drop. The result should be for the pup to drop at once if this stage of his training has been effectively completed. From this point onwards the shot may be used to vary the daily lessons.

The actual introduction to the gun itself should also be carried out with care. It must be remembered that just as the raised hand may appear to a nervous pup as if it were a threatening gesture, so the raised gun may seem as if the handler is threatening him with a stick or fearsome weapon. To start with the pup should be shown the gun, and it should simply be carried under the arm until he is accustomed to it. While the pup is at a distance it may be raised and swung occasionally as if a shot was being fired. Only when the pup is quite accustomed to this should a half-charged cartridge be fired away from the pup. At the sound of the shot he should automatically drop. From then onwards the gun may be substituted for the blank pistol.

It is as well not to teach the pup simply to drop to the sight of the raised gun, as is sometimes advocated, for in that case he may tend to be always looking towards the handler rather than quartering freely. Nor should it be forgotten that a shot fired over the dog's head is much more deafening than one when heard from behind the gun. The same holds good for shots in confined spaces. I have known dogs rendered gun nervous by the owner thoughtlessly firing a shot through a car window at a crow, or else over the head of a young pup on point, in each case nearly deafening the dog. It might also be added that great care should be taken with a .22. The sharp crack of this, like a whiplash, can have a very bad effect on a nervous pup.

The commonest mistakes made by novice handlers in this basic training are not so much from thoughtlessness of this nature as from overkeenness and overtraining. Thus the check cord is used too much, until the pup becomes immune to it and behaves perfectly with it in position, but just as he pleases without it. This unfortunately can happen very easily. The check cord should only be required in the very early stages, and if it is used the pup should, if necessary, be bowled over by it when it is applied, so that the lesson is thoroughly learned without need of repetition. The object of it is primarily to imprint on the pup's mind that the handler has a mysterious means available to control the pup at a distance. Once the pup associates this control with the cord its value as a corrective is lost.

It is desirable that the pup should always feel that the handler has control at all times and every means should be used to foster this illusion. For instance, a fence, or wall, out of doors, or more simply a corridor wall indoors, may be used to force the pup to maintain the correct heel position. Any checks used, such as jerks on the check cord, should be made sufficiently powerful for them not to need to be repeated. Undue use of the check cord, and too frequent awards of tit-bits, are really symptoms of weak handling, and can have just the reverse effect to that intended.

A common resistance encountered by novice handlers is a refusal on the pup's part to come to heel when called. Some undesirable association may have been set up in the pup's mind. One of the most likely reasons for this is that the handler has made the mistake of going towards the pup when he has hesitated about coming to heel. Worse still, he may have been foolish enough to scold, or even punish, the pup for not coming at once. This is quite enough to make the pup associate coming to heel with punishment and so refuse to come.

If the pup does show hesitation about coming to heel when called, the handler should never go towards him. Instead he should promptly turn away from the pup and start walking in the opposite direction. If this does not at once cause the pup to come he should start running, at the same time calling the pup in encouraging tones. Almost certainly this will have the desired effect and cause the pup to give chase. Thereupon he should be encouraged to sit at heel if possible and be made much of before having the lead slipped into place.

Another common resistance which is liable to be encountered by the beginner is a tendency for the pup to refuse to stay put when dropped, but to continue to slide forward in a sitting position, or worse still to get up and move towards the handler. The only real answer in this case is to go back to the beginning and start afresh, for it means in effect that the basic lesson has not been properly learned. The reason may be that the handler has been too keen to get ahead to ensure that the lesson is first thoroughly learned. He may have begun to drop the pup at a distance and called him off the drop too soon, so that he has begun to anticipate the order to move. It should be emphasized again that, in the early stages at least, the handler should always make a point of going to the pup when he has been dropped before giving any further command until he is sure that the pup is absolutely steady and reliable.

In the case of the pup that has developed signs of gun nervousness it is also advisable to go back to the beginning again. It may be that the pup runs away at the sight of the gun or runs to the handler at the sound of the shot. In either event it is better to leave the gun and the blank pistol out of the picture entirely for some time. Only when it is felt that the pup's confidence may have returned and he has had time to forget his fright is it advisable to start again very cautiously.

When persistent and serious resistance of any nature are encountered in training it automatically implies that something is wrong. It is better in such circumstances to discontinue training entirely, even for as long as a month or two, and spend the interval regaining the pup's confidence and studying his temperament. It is almost certain that the early training has been conducted too fast for the pup or that there has been some other basic mistake. The best way to remedy matters is to give the pup time to forget and then start afresh. When training is restarted it is probable that the handler will find the pup more receptive and that he himself has also learned something.

There are those who argue that it is a mistake to start any form of training until the pup is six to nine months old and mature enough to absorb it easily. They maintain that a pup should be allowed a period to grow up in and to play before it is subjected to any intensive training. While I thoroughly agree that it is a mistake to make this preliminary training too intensive, I do not see why the pup should not start learning gently from the time it is weaned. It has been emphasized throughout this book at the risk of boring the reader that the training must always be at the pup's pace and that the handler must never force him too fast. For that very reason it is impossible to lay down any timetables on training. It must vary with each pup and each handler.

The importance of this preliminary training can scarcely be overstressed, and it is therefore well worth while taking plenty of time over it if necessary. Once it has been successfully completed the pup is more than half-way to being a trained dog, for one must assume that he is not lacking in instinct and the rest of his training is largely dictated by instinct. By slowly building up stage by stage on these simple foundations the pup can be trained to perform apparently complex actions, but the basis of the whole method is mutual confidence. Unless both handler and pup have confidence in each other, it is useless to go further, since to do so is like building on sand.

CHAPTER FOUR

INITIAL RETRIEVING

IN THE INITIAL STAGES of retrieving training the aims are comparatively simple. On the command 'Hie lost', or 'Fetch', the pup should go eagerly to fetch the dummy, pick it up cleanly, without mouthing or shaking it and return straight to the handler. He should then deliver it cleanly to hand without fuss on the command 'Dead'. He should learn the meaning of the command 'Mark'. He must also learn to use his nose to find the dummy and his eyes to mark the fall, as well as to follow the handler's directional hand signals for a blind retrieve (i.e. one where he has not seen the dummy thrown).

The very earliest lessons in retrieving may start, as has already been indicated, even before the pup is fully weaned. The instinct to pick up and carry should certainly never be thwarted if it can possibly be avoided. So many cases of difficulty in retrieving must be caused by resistances set up at an early age as a result of thoughtless actions on the part of some human being.

It is natural enough to experience a certain distaste at some of the decaying corpses of long-deceased rats or similar loathsome objects brought proudly up for inspection. Equally trying is the situation when the pup appears triumphantly carrying a precious doll, or delicate pair of nylons, or some such object around the house. The reaction in each case should be to call the pup by name, make much of him, and gently remove the object with the command 'Dead'. To refuse to accept it, or to scold the pup for bringing it, may well be enough to cause him to hesitate about retrieving again. Worse still, to indulge in a tug of war, or chase the pup, may result in him later developing hard mouth or refusing to bring to hand. Naturally enough it is the action of carrying he is liable to connect with the scolding he has received. Why should he doubt that such a delectable object as a decaying rat could be anything but as acceptable to his master as it is to him? By a moment's inattention and lack of thought as to how the pup's mind works his whole training may thus be endangered.

Frequently, however, the owner of a young pup does find himself in a position where not to interfere with the pup's actions might be worse than checking him. This can happen especially easily during the breeding season. A young bird unable to fly is unexpectedly cornered, or an injured bird is trapped fluttering against wire netting, or some similar instance arises where the pup is faced with a wildly struggling and easily damaged animal, before he has fully learned what retrieving is all about. This situation can have far-reaching consequences. On the one hand, the bird may be savaged, and it is even possible the pup may develop the beginnings of hard mouth as a result, having learned that by crunching sharply the struggles of the bird will cease abruptly. Alternatively the youngster may have been actively frightened and may in future be afraid of approaching fur or feather. This may especially be the case if an old cock has clawed a raw youngster with his spurs. Other resistances to retrieving may well develop as a result of such an encounter.

Apart from keeping a look-out for the possibility of any such unfortunate happening and doing his best to avoid it, the handler must simply do his best to minimize the effect if such an encounter does take place. In such circumstances it is always better to check the pup if possible before the situation develops fully. If it has been impossible to prevent the worst and the pup has gone in and killed the bird, the wisest course is to take the pup away from the scene as quickly as possible. Do not make a big scene of it and so imprint it on the pup's mind, but bear in your own mind what has happened and thereafter keep an eye on the pup's future lessons with a view to eradicating any faults which this may have caused.

In practice, as long as this sort of thing is restricted to a solitary occasion, however bad it may have been, little harm will probably have been caused and forgetting it as soon as possible is probably the best policy, or at any rate encouraging the pup to forget it by distracting his mind. If the pup is already retrieving, it may be as well to leave all retrieving severely alone for some time afterwards; even for a matter of weeks or months.

Although the very earliest steps in retrieving may be encouraged by the use of any article to which the pup happens to take a fancy, such as a stick, a piece of rag, or a brush, as soon as the instinct manifests itself clearly a proper dummy should be introduced. I find that a very young pup will frequently take to carrying a toy if he is given one. Since he will in any event supply his own playthings, from leaves to old bones, or possibly more undesirable objects, it is as well to supply something which is not likely to be in any way harmful to him and which it does not matter if he destroys. In this way the instinct to carry can easily enough be encouraged. In a breed where the instinct is in any event natural there is not likely to be much trouble encountered unless a resistance has been set up in one of the ways already mentioned.

In the early stages it may be desirable to provide a small and light weight dummy; from 2–3 lb depending on the breed, but heavy enough to prevent shaking. A sock stuffed tightly with old rags, or cotton waste, or some such material and neatly sewn up is easily enough made. A stuffed roll of canvas, or sail-cloth, is also effective. A lot of people favour stuffed rabbit's skins but I am not personally greatly in favour of them, as there is generally a scent of decay about them unless they have been particularly well preserved, and they can also very easily become brittle. I always feel they may tend to cause mouthing, especially if the dog is later expected to flush game, including fur.

A piece of rubber hosing of fairly large diameter, such as is used in car radiator attachments, is sometimes recommended, and may be useful in the early stages. Unless the ends are blocked and it is weighted, however, it is liable to be too light later on. As well as these some people favour dummies with bird's wings attached, but these are primarily for more advanced retrieving, and it is certainly not advisable to use them in the early stages, as they are liable to cause slovenly retrieving. In any event these are, as I see it, barely worth the trouble involved in making them, since by the time the pup is ready to use them more realistic substitutes can be used to achieve the same effect.

As the pup develops so the size of the dummy should be graded within his powers, but always sufficiently weighty to make him disinclined to try shaking it. Too light a dummy can lead to a spirited pup shaking his head in triumph and inevitably to taking too firm a grip; 3–5 lb should be sufficient, but, of course, in the case of exceptionally powerful young dogs it might even be necessary to make it heavier.

Although only one dummy is used at a time during this stage of the training, it is advisable to make two or three dummies of different kinds which can be used in turn, so that the pup does not become too accustomed only to the one kind. By ringing the changes in this way the pup's interest can be maintained. This is also the first step in teaching the pup that he must be prepared to retrieve anything for which he is sent.

Only the very earliest retrieves of all should be made with the dummy or plaything thrown in full view in the open, so that the pup is encouraged to run in after it at once. Use may here be made of the pup's instinctive reaction to run with any special prize back to his kennel or basket. The handler should place himself in a suitable position with this in mind and then toss the dummy forward in full view of the pup with the command 'Hie lost' or 'Fetch'. Assuming that the pup has rushed after the dummy, which should only have been rolled or bounced in an enticing manner some 6 or 7 ft from him, he will almost certainly pick it up and run back towards his kennel or basket with it. The handler should then intercept him and after making much of him gently remove the dummy with the command 'Dead'.

On no account should the dummy be snatched from the pup, but, while making much of him and encouraging him, it should be gently removed with the command 'Dead'. A slight pressure of the fingers on the jaws will usually suffice to make the pup give up the dummy, but a tug of war should certainly not be allowed to develop, as this is one way to court hard mouth. If he proves reluctant to give it up, a slight pressure of the lips on the teeth should prove enough, while the command 'Dead' is repeated. It is not desirable to offer a piece of biscuit as a reward, as this may come to be expected and the dummy dropped too hastily as a result.

Having successfully allowed the pup to run in after the thrown dummy with the command 'Hie lost', and having had it retrieved to hand, the next stage is to restrain the pup while the dummy is thrown. The dummy may again be thrown in full view, but the pup should not be restrained too long. While he still remains full of eagerness to run after the dummy he should be released with a forward wave and the command 'Hie lost'. From this it is a small step to making him sit while the dummy is thrown before sending him off with a wave of the hand and the command.

As soon as it is clear that the pup understands the general principle the dummy should no longer be thrown so that it lies in full view. It should be thrown to land in grass, where the pup has to use his nose to find it. If the pup is continually allowed to use his eyes only for the retrieve, he will very readily acquire the bad habit of always looking for his retrieves rather than trying to use his nose. He will also tend to rush in on his retrieves and his pick-up will soon become slovenly. He may also in this fashion acquire a dangerous tendency to pounce on the dummy and seize it or play with it. This in turn can lead to mouthing and other faults.

Most people will have seen at some time the wild and inexperienced young dog which at the report of the gun rushes forward in wide circles with his head in the air, looking for something to retrieve rather than using his nose. This is usually caused by careless introduction to early retrieving, and the youngster has become accustomed, after one or two successes, to running in to shot and using his eyes to spot wounded game in front of the gun. Such a dog, by disturbing game over a wide area, brings down curses on the head of his owner, and is in effect worse than useless, whereas with a little care such a state of affairs need never have arisen.

If the pup is forced to use his nose even to a limited extent from the earliest stages he is likely to learn a smooth and controlled pick-up. He is also more likely

Early retrieves from water may involve entering the water to encourage the youngster.

A youngster retrieving a dummy to hand.

to use his eyes to mark the fall of the dummy, which is another point he will find useful subsequently. It might be added that the forward hand wave encouraging the pup to go in the direction of the dummy is the first use of directional hand signals so far.

Once the pup has begun to grasp what is required it is advisable when he returns with the dummy to encourage him to walk at heel for a short while before accepting it from him. In this way he will learn that he must not give it up until he has received the command 'Dead'. If he shows signs of dropping it before he delivers to hand on the command 'Dead', he must be checked verbally and encouraged to continue at heel, still carrying it. After delivering the dummy successfully he should, of course, be made much of verbally.

It should be mentioned here that the handler's attitude towards the dummy is important. He should treat it as if it is something he is really pleased to receive. He must always make much of his dog for retrieving it and let the dog see that he appears to value it. He should also see that it has plenty of his own body scent on it by carrying it inside his coat or in a poacher's pocket. It should never be tainted with petrol, or paraffin, or other scents liable to be unpleasant to the pup's sense of taste, which might lead to mouthing or refusal to pick up. Careless treatment of the dummy is likely to be reflected by the pup. It should scarcely be necessary to add that on no account should the dummy ever be used to punish the pup, even for a token tap to make him sit, as I have seen done. It is by such thoughtless behaviour that resistances to retrieving the dummy are set up.

When the pup fully appreciates the meaning of the command 'Hie lost' a further important step may be taken. The dummy should be dropped in full view of the pup with the command 'Mark'. The handler may then lead him some ten paces away before giving him the command 'Hie lost. Mark', or 'Fetch. Mark'. The pup should at once get the idea and fetch the dummy to hand. On the next occasion the distance may be increased a little and the dummy dropped in a tussock of grass, so that the pup has to use his nose to find it. Should the pup show signs of swanning off past the dummy he should be dropped, and the handler should then get the dummy between him and the pup before recalling the pup towards him and dropping the pup again close to the dummy. He should then be encouraged verbally and made much of when he finds the dummy and brings it to hand.

Some handlers like to develop a special hand signal, such as waving the hand just above the ground, to teach the pup to use his nose to find the dummy. This is usually encouraged in the early stages by throwing a piece of biscuit a few feet away in long grass and encouraging the pup to find it with this signal and the command 'Hie lost'. The dummy is then substituted for the biscuit and a reward given when it is retrieved. Admittedly there are times at field trials when a bird is lying in full view stone dead and is inexplicably apparently without scent. Dog after dog may be tried on it and yet fail to find it. At such times this signal might well be desirable. In general work in the field its utility is more open to question. Such a bird in full view would normally be picked by hand, and if it is not visible the handler is seldom in a position to help the dog. It is difficult to avoid feeling that a dog which needs to look to his handler for this degree of assistance is not using his nose to the full in the first instance, but there may be times when it is useful.

In practice, trained on the lines indicated, the handler should soon find that he is able to take the pup across a field, dropping the dummy on the way with the command

'Mark' and walking as much as a hundred yards, or more, before giving the command 'Hie lost. Mark'. In this way the pup is learning to follow the handler's scent trail and also to get well out on his retrieves from an early age, both of which are excellent grounding for later on. In this and subsequent retrieving he is also likely to be developing his responses to directional hand signals. The hand pointing horizontal from the shoulder to right, or left, or forward, acts as his guide.

From this stage the command 'Mark' may be used whenever the dummy is thrown to be retrieved in the ordinary way. As a further step the pup may be taken out and the dummy thrown as usual. On successfully retrieving it to hand the pup should promptly be taken back to his kennel, or basket. Another dummy may then be hidden in precisely the same place. The pup may then be taken out again and the command 'Hie lost' given from the same position as before. Almost certainly the pup will run to the previous position where the dummy was before and retrieve the fresh dummy without difficulty. Thereafter it is only a matter of pointing in the required direction with the command 'Hie lost' and the pup will realize the dummy is there.

It is important, however, to keep the initial blind retrieves of this nature comparatively simple. The direction of the wind should be such as to make it easy for the pup to find the dummy. Naturally subsequent retrieves will by degrees be made more difficult. By dropping the pup at a distance and then setting him in the required direction by hand signals these lessons can be utilized to make the pup entirely responsive to them. Care must be taken at this stage especially, however, not to overdo the difficulties for an easily discouraged pupil, nor to bore a willing pup.

Signs of rebellion, such as shaking the dummy, refusing

to return with it to hand, mouthing, or returning without the dummy, are typical symptoms of overtraining, if the pup has once performed the lessons perfectly. In such instances rather than try to force the issue and almost certainly be defeated it is better to call the pup in to heel and forget all about those particular lessons for a week or even more. When the dummy is next produced it is probable that all the former keenness will have been regained and the lesson will be performed perfectly. Be warned in time, however, and do not overdo it again.

Some dogs are content to go on with the dummy for a long time. Others will very quickly tire of it. Usually the latter are dogs with instinct well developed who prove admirable in the field later, but are easily bored with substitutes. As with human beings dogs vary, but pointless repetition is boring to the most patient. Although a handler may be keen to demonstrate his pup's performance, he should always be careful of overdoing it.

A fairly common though not particularly serious fault among novice handlers is a tendency to bend down with both hands to receive the dummy from the dog. This is all very well in the early stages of training, but it should be remembered that when actually out shooting it is more probable one hand will be fully occupied with the gun. It may also be that the dog will come to expect this always and will not readily bring the game to hand otherwise. He may even in this way develop a resistance to retrieving to one hand only. On all counts therefore it is preferable to accustom the pup to having the dummy received by one hand only. The other should be used to pat the pup at the same time as a reward whenever possible.

A more serious fault in the novice handler is a tendency to snatch the dummy from the pup. This is probably due to anxiety in case he should drop it and can very readily lead to the pup developing a resistance to retrieving to hand and starting to spit the dummy out before reaching the handler. This same resistance can be caused by the handler staring too hard at the pup as he approaches with the dummy. The situation should not arise, however, if the pup has been encouraged to walk at heel with the dummy before surrendering it on the command 'Dead', as has been recommended.

The best counter if the pup does develop this trait of dropping the dummy is to turn as soon as the pup shows signs of dropping it and walk, or run, in the opposite direction. Even if the pup has dropped the dummy the chances are that he will pick it up again and follow. If he does not do so immediately the command 'Hie lost' should be repeated, and he will then almost certainly pick up the dummy and follow the handler. When the pup does come with the dummy the handler should not at once accept it, but should continue to walk away at speed while encouraging the pup verbally. Once he is certain that it is not going to be dropped, he may slow down and continue to encourage the pup to hold it before finally taking it gently from him with the command 'Dead', while still making much of him at the same time. This should be repeated subsequently until the fault is eradicated completely. Thereafter the handler should take care not to give cause for it to arise again.

Another common resistance which the pup may develop is that of refusing to bring the dummy to hand and circling the handler instead. This can again be caused by staring, but it is probably more often due to a novice handler having made the mistake of scolding the pup on some previous occasion when he has returned with the dummy for running in to fetch it before the command. Instead of associating the scolding with the running in, the pup has naturally associated it with the retrieving to hand, and is thereafter afraid to bring the dummy to hand. The same fault may be seen sometimes in a youngster who has been punished after retrieving for running in to fall of game.

The simplest answer to this problem is to stand with the back to a stone wall. If the pup still refuses to deliver to hand, it may be necessary to stand in a recess where the pup must come direct to the handler. This can readily enough be made by using a gate, or hurdle, in a corner of a field. Alternatively the use of a corridor indoors is quite effective for the same purpose. Once the dummy is delivered to hand the pup should be made much of and encouraged as much as possible.

One of the problems not yet discussed is that of the pup which simply refuses to pick up any dummy or substitute at all. This rooted resistance to retrieving may have been caused in a number of ways already mentioned, but is most probably due to harsh treatment at an early and impressionable age when retrieving some undesirable object. It may well not have been caused by the handler. He may not even know the reason for it, but still be faced with this stubborn resistance. If the pup is kept in the house the importance of first training the household in the rudiments of 'gundog sense' cannot be overstressed.

After every other method has been tried and every dummy, or substitute, offered without success, it may be worth trying the forced-retrieve method. As the name implies, the method involves the use of force and is not to be recommended unless all else fails. It should certainly never be attempted in any event except on a well-grown and mature dog.

The dog's jaws are opened and the dummy slipped inside. He will almost certainly try to spit it out, but should be prevented from doing so. As soon as he ceases to struggle, or object, even for a brief moment or so, the command 'Dead' may be given and the dummy removed, while he is made much of at once. In this way he can be gradually encouraged to associate cause and effect, but it is likely to be a slow process, although generally effective.

A variant of the same principle is that of applying pain, e.g. pinching the dog's ear, while the dog continues to try to spit out the dummy. As soon as the struggles cease so does this application of pain. This principle of distracting the dog's mind from the application of one force by the application of another savours too strongly to my mind of the use of the 'twitch' in shoeing horses. This is a method whereby the horse's muzzle is twisted in a cord tourniquet to distract his attention from the shoeing. Along with the use of spiked collars and other aids to 'breaking' it has no place in modern training methods and should certainly never be applied in the case of a pup.

With one advanced case of refusal to retrieve or even pick up in a mature bitch regarded as incurable at two years of age I was successful with a 'kill-or-cure' method of treatment, consisting of looping a piece of string twice round a dummy and slipping the resulting large loop over her head so that the dummy was held in her mouth like a horse's bit. After a struggle for some minutes while I led her round on a lead, encouraging her verbally, she settled down philosophically and even began to wag her tail. After five minutes I was able to remove the string and thereafter had no further difficulty with her.[1] It must be clear, however, that I am certainly not advocating the use of such measures in the case of a pup. There they would be more likely to cause a resistance to retrieving rather than anything else.

[1] See *Roughshooter's Dog*, Gentry Books.

CHAPTER FIVE

ADVANCED RETRIEVING

THE ELEMENTS OF RETRIEVING have so far been taught with a single dummy, although the actual dummy used may have been of various different kinds. The pup has learned to mark the fall of the dummy, to await the command 'Hie lost', or 'Fetch', depending on which the handler prefers to use, to bring the dummy to hand, and to deliver it on the command 'Dead'. He has also learned to use his nose and to answer hand signals in order to accomplish a blind retrieve. Finally he has learned the meaning of the command 'Mark', and has learned to follow the handler's scent trail to find a dummy dropped at a considerable distance. All the retrieves so far, however, have been comparatively simple and straightforward.

The stage has now been reached where refinements on this training may gradually be introduced to ensure that the pup will be able to cope adequately with every situation which is likely to arise in the shooting field. Although the ultimate training of both dog and handler must be in action in the field it is obviously desirable to prepare the pup for every likely contingency beforehand. The pup should now be ready for this more advanced training.

The difference at this point is that more than one dummy may be used at the same time. The pup must first learn to mark the fall of more than one dummy and to fetch a given one on command. He must also learn that he may not always be required to retrieve, and he must

More advanced retrieving, using a second dummy as a distraction to be ignored. Note the use of the wall behind the handler to ensure a direct retrieve.

Steadying a youngster on point at a dizzied pigeon marked by a twig.

learn to retrieve in spite of distractions such as he may encounter later in the field. He must learn to retrieve from water and cover and over obstacles. Finally he must learn to retrieve dead birds gently, and become accustomed to retrieving all sorts of birds and animals on command, sometimes after having followed a scent trail to find them in the first place while ignoring distractions on the way.

From this stage on the training can be varied more intensively and the pup's interest maintained while the scope of the lessons is greatly widened. From one dummy being thrown, two may be thrown in opposite directions as a first step. The handler may then direct the pup decidedly to one or other dummy, ensuring that he is checked if he shows any tendency to go towards the wrong one. He must then be made much of when he returns with it and, after a brief interval, sent to retrieve the other one. The number of dummies may then gradually be increased.

As a further extension of this lesson the pup may be sent to fetch one dummy to hand signals and made much of when he does so. The handler may then leave him sitting and himself retrieve the second dummy, or alternatively keep him at heel while they go to fetch the second dummy together. In either case the pup should be made much of, as if he had retrieved it. The point it is desired to impress upon him is that he shall not retrieve unless the handler gives the command to do so. It should be remembered never to overdo this repressive training, for it can easily have the opposite effect to that desired and may sour an immature pup. As a general rule, however, any thrown dummy which lands in full view in the open should always, after the initial stages, be picked up by the handler. This will avoid faulty pick-ups caused by over-eagerness and also encourage the pup to ignore easy retrieves close at hand later on in the field.

The pup has already learned the meaning of the command 'Mark'. The dummy should now be thrown with the command 'Mark' and the pup led away from the spot. After a brief interval, on returning to the same place, the command 'Hie lost. Mark' may be given. If the pup fails to remember where the dummy was thrown he may be directed to it by hand signals. In this way, by gradually increasing the number of dummies thrown and the interval elapsing before he is sent to retrieve them, the pup's memory can be exercised. Anyone who has watched a well-trained retriever marking birds at a stand as his master shot them will appreciate the advantage of this memory training.

From this point it is a short step to sending the pup on blind retrieves for several dummies in succession, directing him to each by hand signals. Care must be taken, however, to see that the pup is successful. Too difficult a task may easily sour a willing enough pup. As always throughout the pup's training care should be taken to advance at the pup's pace.

At this stage the pup may be sent on a simple dummy retrieve, either thrown and marked, or blind. On his return towards his handler, triumphantly carrying the dummy, another dummy may be thrown to land in full view some yards wide of him. The handler should be watching him carefully all the time and should he hesitate, as he almost certainly will, or put the dummy down, preparatory to fetching the other, he must be checked with the prohibition 'No'. He should then be encouraged to retrieve the first dummy to hand and made much of when he does so. He may then be sent to retrieve the second dummy, or the handler himself may do so to impress the lesson that the retrieve will never be made without the handler's command.

When the pup has become accustomed to this, and may be relied on to ignore a second dummy thrown while he is returning from a retrieve, another step forward may be taken. A dummy may next be thrown in full view in the open, with the command 'Mark No'. Another dummy may then be thrown in a different direction and the pup sent to fetch it. Yet another dummy may then be thrown, but any attempt to retrieve the first dummy must be firmly checked. The lesson that the handler must always give the command to retrieve will thus be further emphasized, but once again it should be stressed that such repressive training should not be attempted until the pup is mature enough to accept it readily.

The introduction of another type of dummy, rolled to simulate a running hare, or rabbit, may be useful at this stage. An old croquet ball, or bowl, studded with three or four football-boot studs and several hare or rabbit tails, bounces along in a highly attractive and teasing manner, just like a rabbit zigzagging in cover. Almost as effective is a sawn log of wood about 6 inches in diameter and 2 or 3 inches across, or even a suitably knobbly-shaped turnip. All are easily obtained and are not meant to be retrieved, being only used as a distraction when the pup is in the act of retrieving a dummy to train him in steadiness.

The pup's initial reaction to this new innovation is likely to be one of surprise and he may well be tempted to give chase. If necessary, the check cord may be introduced, but it should not be required. If the new type of dummy is at first thrown well wide of the pup it should be possible to check him verbally should he show any tendency to go after it. Once again it is a question of gauging the pup's capabilities and not overstraining them.

In a short while the handler should find that he can throw several dummies in different directions and then set the pup on to each in turn. At the same time he will be able to bowl these rolling dummies directly across the path of the returning or departing pup and no notice should be taken of them. It may be added that care must be taken not to hit the pup with one of these dummies accidentally, as not unnaturally this could have a very bad effect and might even set up a resistance to retrieving, or cause the pup to avoid returning straight to the handler.

In this manner by degrees the pup's confidence in his handler and his own powers can be steadily increased. The pup should have a genuine and obvious zest for retrieving, but he can still easily be bored by an unimaginative handler. From this point onwards, however, the lessons should increasingly bear a resemblance to work in the shooting field, and it should not be found at all difficult to vary the lessons each day and thus maintain both the handler's and the pup's interest. An assistant throwing the dummy can be a big help at this stage, either to distract the pup as it returns, or to throw the dummy from a concealed position at gradually extended distances. The handler may also start to fire a blank shot in the direction of the dummy, ensuring that the pup drops to the sound while still marking the fall. Alternatively some trainers favour a dummy launcher, which can be bought in most gunsmiths. These have a special hollow dummy, which fits over the launcher tube, and when fired send the dummy anything up to fifty yards or more in the direction to which it is pointed. They can be useful in advanced training, but are really of most use to the professional trainer with a number of pups to train. Some trainers do not favour the canvas covered hollow dummy that has perforce to be used and, although they can be helpful on

Teaching the drop to shot and flush by pulling the slate back to release the bird (distance reduced for photography).

Mr Ian Glass's F.T. Champion Labrador bitch Blakemere Mega of Garleton retrieving a live cock pheasant runner to hand.

occasions, they are expensive. There can be little doubt that an assistant working in conjunction with the trainer is very much preferable.

The pup may now be taught to deal with the various obstacles which he is likely to encounter, from gates and hedges to wire fences and stone walls. Here there must, of course, be some variations between breeds, and some pups may have to be taught to find their way round or through the obstacles rather than over them. In the early stages, at any rate, only comparatively simple obstacles should be chosen which are easily within the pup's powers. The dummy should be thrown over the obstacle while the pup watches. The command 'Hie lost. Over' may then be given. As the pup proves able to face them the difficulties of the obstacle may be increased.

The same steady approach is desirable in the matter of facing water and cover. As with willingness to retrieve, so willingness to face cover and a liking for water are to some extent inherited qualities, but most gundogs can be encouraged to face cover and all gundogs can swim if necessary. In the first instances small patches of cover should be chosen. It may even be felt necessary to build one or two artificial clumps on the lines of those illustrated. In most cases the dummy thrown, or placed, in a clump of natural cover will be sufficient for a start. From small and easy beginnings the pup can be encouraged to face rougher cover in search of the dummy. If his keenness has been maintained and gauged correctly, all will be well.

An inherited liking for water, of course, makes the question of teaching the pup to face water perfectly simple. Even so it is desirable to make the approach a gradual one. It is obviously preferable to make a start, if possible, in midsummer when the water is warm rather than in mid-winter when the water is freezing. To begin with, the pup should be introduced to shallow water with a gradual sloping bank. Some pups will simply revel in it at once and then there should be no difficulty. Others may be reluctant to enter it at first. In that case it may be advisable to throw the dummy into shallow water, or if the lie of the land makes it suitable, over shallow water, so that the pup has to cross it in order to retrieve.

The next stage is to choose some water where the pup will have to swim a little, taking care that the entrance and exit banks are easy and that the water is shallow at first. The dummy may then be thrown either over or into the water and the pup encouraged to swim for it. On his return he should be made much of and encouraged. In this way he should soon become an accomplished water dog.

Resistances to water can, however, be set up in a number of ways by a thoughtless handler, even where the pup is naturally a keen water dog. Ice on the water, too strong a current, underwater obstacles, too steep or slippery a bank, or similar causes are enough to give an adult dog a severe fright and cause him to be chary of entering water again, let alone a pup. Quite apart from the danger of an inexperienced pup being drowned, any of these are fully enough to cause a resistance to facing water.

The only way to overcome such a resistance is by the use of kindness and a gradual approach. The example of other dogs, or the sight of his handler wading across water himself, or even swimming, may be sufficient to overcome his initial fear, but it may well be a lengthy process. If the pup proves extremely frightened of water it is as well to assume that he has had an early scare and treat him with especial care. It should scarcely need to be added that any attempt to force the issue by throwing the pup into the water, or badgering him to enter, is likely to have the opposite effect to that desired.

Once the pup is thoroughly accustomed to water the obeying of hand signals while in the water can be added to his other accomplishments. This is easily enough done in a pond or reasonably large stretch of water by sending the pup on a blind retrieve. If to begin with he does not see the dummy floating on the water, it may in the early stages be permissible to throw a stone to attract his attention to the splash. By this time, however, he should be sufficiently responsive to whistle and to signal to be set directly on to the dummy in the water.

It is at this stage in the pup's education that some handlers advocate using a winged dummy to encourage the pup to pick up his game correctly. I cannot really see that a great deal is to be gained by this in practice. To my mind as efficient a way is to start the pup on a dead duck. With the wings and head securely held in place by a broad rubber band made from a car inner tube it should make a compact bundle easily retrieved.

It is important that the duck should be reasonably freshly killed, but not warm and bloody. There should equally be no question of using a deep-frozen bird, icy cold and solid, or one which has been dead for several days and is now distinctly high and tainted. Any of these could readily cause mouthing or refusal to retrieve. An advantage of the duck is that, being a close-feathered bird, no loose feathers, which might also cause mouthing and a distaste for retrieving, are likely to be encountered. For this last reason a pigeon is not a good bird to use for these early retrieving lessons, nor do I like the principle of slipping it inside a nylon stocking, as is sometimes advocated, since this is easily snagged and simply is not realistic.

Before sending the pup on such a retrieve it is advisable

first to show him an example of what he is now going to be expected to find and retrieve. Otherwise he may quite easily ignore the bird and persist in looking for one of the dummies which he has hitherto retrieved. It should also be remembered that the pup ought not to be asked to retrieve any one duck more than once, although the same bird may be used for more than one dog and may in the first instance have been retrieved by another dog. Use of the same bird several times with the same dog may lead to mouthing or refusal to retrieve. In any event two or three successful retrieves of this kind should be all the introduction that the youngster should require.

From this point onwards it is desirable to vary the bird retrieved. A crow is a tight-feathered bird, which is apparently not pleasant to taste. Although for this reason it is not a good thing to use in the earliest instances, it is all to the good once the youngster understands what is required and is gaining experience. Starlings are another unpleasant-tasting mouthful and are also good training outside the shooting season. If the youngster is given this sort of varied experience from the early stages, there should later on be no trouble with woodcock, which some dogs dislike intensely and refuse to carry.

The next stage is the laying of a scent trail. This is virtually the final stage of training before the youngster is ready for the real thing. Although it would probably be perfectly feasible to shoot over the youngster at this stage, and indeed no harm might result, at the same time his education is not completed. By teaching him to follow a scent trail his retrieves in the field are likely to be far more polished and effective than if he has to learn by experience to use his nose to puzzle out the scent of a wounded bird.

There are several ways of laying a trail. Most commonly perhaps a duck with pinioned wings is used to lay a natural trail or else an artificial trail is laid either with the aid of an assistant, by means of a fishing rod, or with a length of fishing line. It is undesirable for the handler simply to walk along the line towing a bird behind him, as the pup will almost certainly then merely follow the handler's scent instead of the scent of the bird. On several occasions at field trials where a bird or rabbit has been laid in cover for an artificial retrieve I have seen a dog follow the line of the steward and claim the man and his bag of game. Such a reaction is reasonable enough, and it is desirable to avoid any similar confusion in the youngster's mind.

When an assistant is available it is all quite simple. In order to avoid the pup following the handler's scent a freshly shot bird should be suspended between two pieces of fishing line each at least 30 yds long. The handler and his assistant then take an end apiece and by dragging the bird along the ground the trail is laid. At the end of the trail it is probably advisable to lift the battered and bedraggled bird and replace it with a fresh one.

The youngster may now be taken to the spot. He may then either be set on the trail direct as a blind retrieve or a shot may be fired and a dummy thrown elsewhere. He may then be directed away from the dummy and on to the prepared trail. The scent in this first instance should have been sufficiently strong and the trail sufficiently easy to ensure success. On retrieving the bird he should, of course, be made much of and encouraged verbally.

Without an assistant a trail may be readily enough laid by using a bait-casting rod and a weight and casting a line some 30 or 40 yds. Making a suitably wide detour, the handler may then attach the bird to the end and wind it in, thus laying an effective enough trail. Alternatively, leaving the line free on the reel, he can walk with it as far as he wishes before setting it down with the bird attached. On returning to the rod he must then walk in a semicircle with the bird as the centre point. When he is sure that he is completely free of his own scent trail he can then wind in the bird and lay the trail. This latter simple method can, of course, be used with a reel and line alone, but the rod will probably be found useful for lifting the line above small obstacles or snags on the way.

It is important to make these early scent trails easy enough for the pup to puzzle them out without difficulty. Subsequent trails may be made as easy or as difficult as is wished, although as ever, the youngster's progress should be the guide. With the help of an assistant the bird can be lifted and breaks in the trail simulated before continuing the trail either up or down wind.

Although it may sometimes be advisable to assist the youngster if he shows signs of losing heart, once he is on the trail the handler should do his best not to interfere. There will almost certainly be times when the handler must check the pup and set him right, but in practice in the field he should remember that nine times out of ten the dog will be right and the handler wrong. The object of this training is primarily to teach the youngster to work out a scent trail for himself rather than learn the bad habits of turning always to his handler for instructions when he should be relying on his own instinct. Since the handler knows the intricacies of the trail he has laid, he will find this an extremely useful means of assessing accurately his dog's capabilities. He will also probably learn something about the problems of scent and scenting in the process.

The lessons have now reached the stage where the pup is ready for the shooting field. Without any game actually being shot over him, and without being allowed to run into undue temptation, the pup should now have attained a considerable degree of steadiness. It merely remains to make sure that the lessons learned are carried out in practice and that the dog is not inadvertently spoiled in the early stages of field work. To this end it is desirable that the first birds shot over the youngster should not necessarily all be retrieved. It is also naturally undesirable that he should have badly shot or merely winged specimens to start with in the field, even though he might prove capable of retrieving them well to hand.

There should certainly be no panicky dispatches after wounded game, which can undo all that has been learned. A certain degree of care is necessary for the pup's first season, and it is as well to start with easy work, even if the dog is capable of more. Both the pup and the handler should be learning each other's ways and continuing to learn to work together. Careless handling in the field, it should once again be emphasized, can quickly ruin a well-trained dog.

Throughout these chapters on retrieving there has been little direct mention made of hard mouth. The stress has been on prevention rather than cure. Once the youngster has developed the habit of 'closing the suitcase' on his retrieves there is little that can be done about it. The advocates of hedgehogs in rabbit skins, thorns, or barbed wire in dummies, or knitting-needles thrust through game, may all effect temporary cures, but they are unlikely to be anything more. A retriever which habitually brings back his birds with the ribs broken and mangled is worse than useless. To a certain extent hard mouth may be hereditary, but undoubtedly more dogs are allowed to become hard mouthed through bad or just careless training than were ever born hard mouthed.

It has been emphasized that the pup should not be allowed to mouth or shake the dummy, or become slovenly about picking up through running in to retrieves lying in the open. It has also been stressed that the approach to retrieving should be gradual, starting with a close-feathered bird such as a duck. An inexperienced pup should not be allowed to retrieve a wounded bird until sufficiently trained. Mouthing freshly shot and bloody game can also readily lead to the pup 'closing the suitcase' on birds struggling in his jaws. Carelessness in any of these respects and panicky dispatches in the field can lead from bad to worse.

At the same time it is not the end of the world if a pup does commit some apparent and glaring error once; even starting to eat a bird, as a pup of mine did once in full view at a Field Trial. Then the best answer is to lay off all retrieving for several weeks and allow the incident to be forgotten. After that, start afresh, if necessarily right back at the beginning again. In the case mentioned I did not allow the pup to retrieve another partridge until the following season. She never offered to repeat the fault and has a particularly soft mouth. The fault was mine for putting her in for too long a day too young and the Trial Steward's for allowing a badly mangled bird to be used for a retrieve in a Puppy Stake.

It must also be remembered that there are exceptions to every rule. The dog which can retrieve an egg unbroken is not necessarily soft mouthed on birds. Some people maintain that their dogs can kill rats without it affecting their retrieving and, although I certainly do not advocate it, I have seen retrievers of which this was quite true. Admittedly plenty of dogs are hard on fur and soft on feather. I even know one dog which regularly crunches a bird on the first day of the season and is perfectly all right thereafter. Different people inevitably have different standards of what is hard mouthed, but trained on the lines indicated the handler should obtain the best from his pup.

CHAPTER SIX

HUNTING, QUARTERING, POINTING

THEORETICALLY AT LEAST gundogs may be divided into two large natural groups, namely foot scenters, i.e. retrievers and spaniels, on the one hand, and air scenters, i.e. pointers and setters, on the other. Like many other theories, in practice the distinction is non-existent, since there are times when any dog may be following either foot scents or air scents. Some retrievers and spaniels on obtaining an air scent can point as well as any setter, and when pointers are 'roading out' a scent after a covey has flown they are, in fact, following foot scent.

The important distinction is one of range. The question is whether the dog will be expected always to hunt within gunshot or whether he will be expected to hunt beyond gunshot. If the dog is to hunt beyond gunshot, he must obviously point, or clearly game is liable to be flushed without being shot. It is possible, as in the case of pointer-retrievers, that the dog may be expected at times to hunt outside gunshot and at other times within gunshot. It is in any case desirable that a well-trained dog should be able to vary his pace and his range according to command and the requirements of the ground. Most experienced dogs do learn to vary their range with the scenting conditions and the nature of the ground in any case, but this can be taught, and it is advisable that it should be.

The dog which ranges always within gunshot may flush the game without warning, but should then drop automatically. The dog which ranges beyond gunshot must point when he finds the game. He may then be taught to flush the game on command, or the handler may flush the game, but on the game being flushed he must then also drop automatically. The training in either case is not so very different basically.

Once the pup has been thoroughly grounded in preliminary obedience training it is possible to start training him to quarter his ground and instil the ideas of range which will subsequently be required. This is largely a matter of experience. The pup should always be sent off to one side or the other with a wave of the hand and the command 'Cast on'. If he shows signs of circling back, he must be urged forward by hand signals, and the handler may, if necessary, turn towards him for this purpose. In the early stages the direction of march is not important and may be very erratic, but the pup should never be allowed to quarter behind the handler.

If the pup is not required to hunt more than 20 yds or so either side of the handler, he will not be expected to range forward much more than 5 or 10 yds. It is perfectly feasible to teach these range limits by means of a light check cord. In a very short space of time by this means the pup will accustom himself to the range which is intended.

The youngster who is expected to range some 60 yds either side of the handler is another matter. Although his range forward should be only half as much (i.e. some 30–40 yds), here control must be by whistle and the preliminary training must be sound. The pup must be sent off with a wave of the hand and the command 'Cast on'. When he reaches the limit of his range the handler should attract his attention with a short blast on the whistle and recall him, either by signal or whistle, and then cast him in the opposite direction by signal. To start with it may be necessary to change direction frequently to bring the pup across more readily, but for a pup with the instinct to range ahead this training is merely exploiting natural instinct. The control here is at a distance reminiscent of sheepdog training and accordingly the preliminary training must have been thoroughly absorbed.

In the case of a pup used as a pointer-retriever it is desirable to train him to have two distinct ranges. He should be able to range wide in the open when required and also adapt himself to ranging within gunshot when the cover is thicker and when his ability to point is of no advantage to his handler. In such a case it is advisable to start the youngster with wide ranging and bring him in closer afterwards. It is easy enough to bring him in once he has been accustomed to wide ranging, but it is a different matter training a pup to range wide when he has only been allowed previously to range within gunshot.

Once repressive training of this nature has been effective it is never easy to introduce alternatives. The best way to extend a youngster's range when he shows no inclination to range wide is probably with the aid of an assistant. The dog should then be encouraged to range between the handler and the assistant, being called by each in turn as they slowly widen the gap between them.

To a certain degree each dog should have a variable range. At least the speed at which the pup ranges must to some extent be governed by the nature of the ground, by scenting conditions, by the dog's physical proportions and by individual ability. As the dog learns to differentiate between scents, and as the nature of the ground and scenting conditions vary, clearly his pace should also vary. At the same time obviously there are bound to be very considerable variations between, for instance, a cocker and a Gordon setter, and there will be almost as great variations between dogs of the same breed. The essential points are that each dog should learn to hunt his ground adequately, not missing any game, at the greatest speed he is capable of achieving under the conditions prevailing at the time.

An important point to remember always when training a pup in quartering is that he is covering a lot of ground. Unless he is well grown and physically fit it is easy to overdo it. While the handler is only covering a few hundred yards the youngster may be covering a mile. Ten minutes at a time should be quite enough for young pups. Much more and they are liable to turn into slow potterers before they have even started. An obvious 'merriness' and zestful style is a joy to watch in any dog setting about his work, but by keeping him too hard at it too young this can readily enough be drained out of him and become replaced by a slow deadened response to hand signals.

Training the pup to quarter adequately and teaching the required range should be a comparatively simple matter, although rather a lengthier process in the case of the variable-range variable-pace pointer-retriever. The important part of this training is making sure that the pup becomes responsive to game scents and to the sight of game flushing in front of him. He must learn to distinguish between cold scents and fresh scents. He must learn to differentiate between the scents of dead and wounded and live game. He must learn to use the wind and range accordingly. Naturally experience in the field is helpful here, and this cannot all be learned at once, but most of the basic essentials can be taught under prepared conditions. It is clearly better that they should first be learned where there is an element of control if possible, rather than the matter left largely to chance.

It must be appreciated that this training does not

necessarily follow on in sequence with the retrieving training outlined in the previous chapters, even where both are applicable to the youngster. It may be concurrent with the retrieving training, or it may even come first. It is impossible to give more than an outline of training methods, and their application must vary with each pup and each handler.

From the earliest stages when the pup is allowed to roam freely there can be no harm in accustoming him to hand signals and giving him some idea of quartering and range, although again it should be stressed that intensive training should not be attempted too young. It is desirable in any event to start training the pup to quarter his ground before he has been taught to jump obstacles. In this way there is less likelihood of his developing the bad habit of breaking fence, i.e. leaving the field he is working in with the handler without command. In some places it may well be that the nature of the fields is such that they can be used to teach the pup the limits of his range. In other words, on reaching the hedge he may be turned and brought back by whistle or signal. His response to hand signals and whistle naturally dictate the ease, or otherwise, of this training.

In practice it is almost certain that this training will at least in part be concurrent with the retrieving training, or in some cases earlier. There is, however, one big difference between retrieving training and training to hunt. Retrieving may be taught almost entirely with the dummy or by artificial means. Only the early stages of the training to hunt can be satisfactorily taught without at least artificial substitutes for live game. In the later stages the training must be on live game, even if it is artificially introduced to the ground. To complete the pup's education on scents and scenting ground with a plentiful supply of game is almost an essential.

The rolling dummy made from a croquet ball, or sawn log of wood, or a knobbly turnip, may be utilized in this training also, but with a difference. In the retrieving training it was important that the pup learned to continue with his retrieving in spite of the distraction of the dummy. In this training whenever the dummy is rolled it should be greeted with a shot and the pup should at once be dropped.

An assistant concealed behind a tree or hedge down wind of the pup is useful here. From this concealed position, when the handler fires a blank the assistant can bowl one of these rolling dummies past the pup. To start with it is advisable to make sure that the pup is dropped and that he is well under control. Should he show any desire to give chase, resort may have to be made to the check cord, but if the training has been gauged correctly it should not be necessary. As an alternative to the rolling dummy an ordinary dummy thrown by the assistant may also be used. When the pup has obediently dropped to shot and the sight of the dummy in the air in front of him he may, if desired, be sent to retrieve it. Gradually the shot may be omitted and the pup dropped simply to the sight of the dummy in the air or on the ground in front of him.

The use of a rabbit pen if one is available is an advantage in some ways, but by no means a necessity, and in some ways better dispensed with altogether, except by the professional trainer who has a number of pups to train on quickly. The youngster can be taught there to drop automatically at the sight of rabbits and he can readily be trained to hunt them out of cover. There is, however, more than a grain of truth in the old chestnut about the trainer whose rabbits became so accustomed to the proceedings that whenever he blew the whistle to drop a pup the rabbits also dropped.

Carefully used a rabbit pen can be useful in training a dog to ignore rabbits completely. Injudiciously used it can, like injudicious use of the check cord, have little or no effect in that the youngster behaves perfectly in the rabbit pen, but runs riot after rabbits outside. For the amateur handler training his own dog, as good results should be obtainable by using the dummy rolled in front of the pup and by careful introduction to live game in suitable natural or artificial cover.

From the rolling dummy it is a brief step to teaching the pup to drop to flushed birds. A friend with a dovecote, or a loft of homing pigeons, is an asset. A dovecote in the garden is even more convenient. Resort can then be made to a method first used, as far as I know, by General W. N. Hutchinson in the last century, but still none the less effective.

On the ground the pup is to hunt, two or three small holes about 6 inches across by 10 inches long should be dug. In each of these a pigeon can be placed and covered with a slate. Attached to the slate should be a length of fishing line tied to a marker stuck in the ground. As the pup approaches the spot where a pigeon is hidden the handler simply pulls the fishing line attached to the marker and pulls back the slate releasing the pigeon which flies up in front of the dog in the manner of flushed game. A blank can then be fired and the pup dropped. In practice he is quite likely to drop at first out of sheer surprise at the sudden appearance of the bird, but in this way he is likely to become used to dropping automatically at the sight of flushed game.

Teaching the pup to point is another matter altogether. Here, as in retrieving, instinct may be so deeply ingrained and so strong in the pup that he is pointing instinctively almost from the moment he is weaned. As in retrieving, the best thing to my mind is to encourage instinct when it shows rather than ignore it and possibly allow resistances to be set up. Even if the instinct does not manifest itself strongly most pups can with patience be taught to point reasonably well.

In the case of a pup which starts standing still and stiffening at the first sight of strange objects the rest is usually easy. Where there is no instinct shown it may be either desirable to wait until it manifests itself or until it is felt the time is ripe for this training. Whatever the case recourse must be once again made to the dovecote, for this is a part of the training which cannot be taught without the use of live game.

To simulate the presence of live game in front of the pup when it is quartering it is necessary, as with teaching the reaction to flushing game by General Hutchinson's method, to prepare the ground. The pigeon under the slate may be used, but the scent is liable to be weak. The use of the game in cages is another method sometimes used, but again the scent is liable to be poor. To my mind the most satisfactory method is simply the dizzied or locked pigeon, or gamebird. As it will be expected to fly away, the use of a homing pigeon is an advantage, since it can be used time after time.

The process of dizzying game is quite simple. The bird's head is tucked beneath its wing as for sleep and the bird is gently rocked several times between the hands. It is then laid on the ground very gently, lying on its back with its head still tucked beneath its wing. If the head comes out the probability is that the bird will still lie in that position for five or six minutes. If the head remains under the wing the bird may remain for a quarter of an hour or longer.

The process of locking the bird is even easier. The head is tucked under the wing, which is then stretched downwards in front of the near leg and the tip thrust very carefully behind the far leg. The bird is then very gently placed down in a standing position with its head still beneath its wing, and it will remain locked there indefinitely.

The secret in both cases lies in placing the bird on the ground with great care, if possible laying it against a tuft of grass to hold the head and neck in position. If several pigeons are being laid it is as well to mark the position of each with a twig stuck in the ground as a marker, so that the handler can recognize when the pup is approaching them well in advance and prepare accordingly.

In the first instance it may be advisable to bring the pup up carefully in a controlled approach on the check lead from down wind. As soon as the pup shows the slightest sign of having winded the bird it is important to check him. He should then be gently and slowly stroked all over his body while the handler remains absolutely still beside him. If the handler feels that the pup's response is insufficient to be sure that he is scenting the bird, he may allow him to advance slowly until he is sure he must be. Then he must once again freeze beside the dog and merely stroke him slowly over the neck and body.

The first few attempts may be disappointing, but the handler must try to communicate his desire for the pup to remain still by remaining still himself. I know one very able trainer who goes to the extent of getting down on his hands and knees and freezing beside his pup. Others hold their pup in the classic show position, with one hand holding the tail and the other the head or a forepaw. Generally it is enough simply to remain bent over the pup with one hand slowly stroking him until he freezes.

If the bird being used should get up and fly away

during the lesson, the pup should honour the flush by dropping. If the pup has truly stiffened on point, then the handler may well hold the point until the bird does fly, making sure that the pup then drops. Once the pup has really stiffened he will probably at first be deaf to all else. This is all to the good and should be encouraged in the early stages. Thereafter the pup should always be a staunch pointer.

Certain breeds, setters especially, are liable to lie down on point. This is probably an inherited trait from the days when they were trained to find game for bird netters and then lie down while the net was drawn over them. Pointers, which were primarily used for hawking, were not expected to do this and probably this is why they are less liable to lie down on point. As the dog may be lost to sight in any sort of long grass or heather if he lies down on point, this is clearly an undesirable trait, and if the pup attempts to lie down on point he should be gently checked from doing so.

When the pup comes on point the handler should not immediately rush up behind him. This is liable to cause him to draw forward or alternatively look round at the handler and break his point. The approach should be made slowly from the side and the pup may be spoken to gently with the command 'Steady' if it is felt necessary and if he attempts to draw on. In any case the pup should never be harshly spoken to or roughly handled on point, as this may cause him to blink, or come off point. The same result may be caused by working a young dog with an older dog too soon.

To start with naturally the youngster should always be worked directly into the wind to make matters easier both for him and his handler. The handler will probably be surprised on occasions when he appreciates the distances at which his dog has been able to scent game.

Distances of a hundred yards and more are not uncommon. Once he is a reliable pointer, however, the youngster must learn to work correctly with a cheek wind or down wind.

With a cheek wind the correct method of working is for the dog to work at an angle to the handler's line of advance, so as to cover the maximum of ground without disturbing game. Working down wind he should make a sweep forward and work his way back towards the handler. In this way some game may unavoidably be flushed, but the dog will be working his ground correctly. If he is restricted in range and merely used at close range down wind, then his pointing ability is not being utilized.

It may be necessary to cast the dog firmly forward in the desired direction both for a cheek wind and downwind conditions in the earliest stages, but an intelligent youngster will soon understand what is required and why. In most cases it will probably follow instinctively when the instincts to hunt and point have been correctly developed. I have seen dogs which instinctively knew how to work such conditions, although their handlers were not aware that what they were doing was correct. If any game is flushed out of range during these early lessons, the handler must be prepared to accept it philosophically.

In practice the handler will learn much about scents and scenting at this stage by watching his dog's reactions and he will also learn much about his dog's capabilities and nose. The faint wag of the tail acknowledging the scent of a covey of partridges which departed as the handler entered the field, the brief check at a hare's form still warm with the imprint of the occupant, the drop of the head to examine a recent foot scent, and the raised head testing the air preparatory to the point, all these and many more signs tell their story to the observant handler as he watches his dog. He will find that it pays to watch his dog constantly and learn to interpret these signs correctly.

Whether the youngster is desired to flush the game or whether the handler is content to do so himself must depend on how the dog is going to be used. Once the dog is staunch on point in any event it is advisable to take him over some likely ground where game is known to be lying, so that he may have the chance to find and point the real thing. Whether he is brought up under control on the check lead or whether he is quartered freely over the ground must depend on the degree of training and staunchness his handler feels he has achieved. Once the point is made the handler may gently urge the pup forward, walking beside him slowly and encouraging him verbally to draw on, until the birds are flushed with the command 'Set up'. The likeness to the command 'Sit' in any event is likely to make the pup drop, even if the sight of the birds being flushed does not cause him to do so. In due course the command 'Up' by itself should be enough to cause the dog to drop.

Thus far the handler has flushed the birds simply by the sound of his voice. In order to train the pup to flush the birds himself, a dizzied, or locked, pigeon may be used. The pup should be brought up on point from an up-wind position under control. In this way the pup is likely to come on point rigidly right over the bird. After a few moments on point the pup should then be urged forward with the command 'Set up'. The handler should be alongside him in a position to control matters and urge him forward.

In the first instances it may be advisable to flush the bird at the same instant, either with the foot, or by hand, or with the check cord. Should the pup attempt to mouth the bird, or pick it up, the prohibition 'No' must be used firmly and the bird allowed to fly off as the pup drops. If necessary a piece of string may be loosely looped round the jaws as a temporary muzzle while the dog is on point. If it is used it should at once be removed, when the bird has been flushed, but by then the lesson will probably have been learned. With a little care the youngster can be taught to flush the dizzied bird without any attempt to mouth it. In this way he will learn to get his nose under game rather than 'peg' it. In practice on most occasions in the field the game will have been flushed before the dog has had time to reach it, but he must learn that he should not attempt to retrieve it, even if he is in a position to do so, as when working in cover. Such cover work in suitable natural or artificial cover should not be taught to a pointing dog until staunch, being contrary to the pointing training.

From this stage onwards the lessons merge increasingly with work in the field and the dog is now almost as far advanced as the handler can help him to be without shooting over him. Already, however, the handler will have had plenty of occasions to judge how he is developing. He will have seen his quartering develop stylishly. He will have seen him suddenly check in mid-stride and turn rigidly on point. The handler cannot expect a picture-book stance on every occasion. Sometimes it will be perfect, with head, body and tail in a straight line, and forepaw raised for feather, or hind for fur, but it is just as likely to be with all four paws on the ground and the head back almost over the shoulder as a scent is nearly overshot. Whatever the position the point is always an arresting spectacle, and if when the game is flushed, either by the handler or the dog, the pup then drops automatically, the handler will feel already that his training has been worth while.

CHAPTER SEVEN

BRACE WORK AND GENERAL

WHERE TWO DOGS ARE WORKED together the results should always appear more impressive to the onlooker even when the work itself is not necessarily outstanding. The sight of two dogs hunting their ground independently of each other, crossing in front of the handler, is always a pleasing spectacle. When both dogs drop together at flush, or stiffen on point simultaneously, one backing the other, it is a delight to watch. Finally, when one is sent on a retrieve in one direction and the other on another bird in another direction, and each returns promptly and triumphantly to bring their birds to hand, what handler can fail to feel a pleasant glow of satisfaction? He has good reason to do so, for training two dogs to work together is not as simple a matter as training only one dog.

Probably the soundest way to set about training two dogs to work as a pair is to take two well-matched youngsters and train both of them on. This is not quite as simple as it sounds, since it is not generally a good plan to train them together. Very much better results are likely to be obtained if they are trained separately and if each is more or less a trained dog before they are taken out as a pair together. To start with, then, the handler will find that working two dogs in itself requires a great deal more vigilance and care than merely working one alone. Until he becomes accustomed to watching more than one dog at a time and consciously looking ahead he is likely to find a variety of faults arising.

So far no mention has been made of the common situation where there is more than one dog in the household, even if only one is a gundog. Whether they are of the same breed and the same sex, or whether they are different in every way, one golden rule should always be observed. There should never be any favouritism shown between them. However many dogs are kept, the same rule holds good, otherwise kennel jealousy can lead to endless trouble both in training and in work.

To a certain extent kennel jealousy is almost certain to arise if a youngster is introduced into a household where there has only been one dog previously. Naturally the newcomer will be resented. In order to counter this and soften the blow a little it may well be advisable to introduce a companion of the opposite sex, even though this in itself introduces inevitably the problem of a mixed kennel. Unless it is desired to mate them it is as well to bear this point in mind. Whatever their sexes there is almost bound to be an initial clash of wills, even if it is very brief and results in the newcomer's abject surrender. It is as well to keep an eye on the proceedings, but allow matters to run their natural course if possible. Interference is only likely to add fuel to the fires of jealousy.

When it comes to training it is not usually advisable to train the younger dog with the older dog present. Occasionally an older dog may be useful to teach an example to the youngster, and kennel jealousy can sometimes be utilized by an experienced trainer to overcome a resistance (e.g. where one dog refuses to retrieve, the example of a kennel rival may persuade him to do so), but care must be exercised. Simply to take the youngster out with an older dog and expect him to learn by example is asking for trouble. Either the youngster may run wild and encourage the older dog to do so, too, or possibly the youngster may come to rely so completely on the older dog that he becomes unable to work by himself. Worst of all, the youngster is liable to learn all the older dog's bad habits. He may become pottery and slow, or wild and ill behaved. It is also as well to remember that in the house a gundog may easily learn the house manners of a lap dog.

Admittedly there are times when a well-trained old dog can be used to give the youngster confidence, as, for instance, when entering water. He may also at times be used as an example at the handler's discretion. When, for instance, there is persistent trouble with retrieving, as noted above, kennel jealousy may be a powerful weapon if there is suitable opportunity to employ it. The handler must make his own observations and act accordingly. Nor should he forget that it is a two-edged weapon and may well be the cause of resistance to training.

If two dogs are to be used together, however, any traces of kennel jealousy must be eradicated, or kept sternly under control. Faults like seizing game retrieved by another dog, running in to shot to prevent another dog retrieving, refusing to back another dog on point and similar faults can result from uncontrolled jealousy. They can be extremely tiresome. Although two dogs can and should be a pleasure to work with, in such circumstances they are worse than useless.

It is advisable, as has already been pointed out, not to try to introduce dogs to brace work until they are reasonably mature and their training has been more or less completed. Otherwise it is likely that one dog will quickly establish a moral ascendancy over the other. The more experienced will tend to lead and the other follow. The same thing is liable to arise where one dog is lazy and the other energetic, and it is always to be avoided in

Shooting on the moor, over a brace of pointer-retrievers.

A brace of grouse being retrieved to hand.

brace work. To start with, therefore, it is always advisable to try to match a pair of dogs for brace work as nearly as possible for size and temperament and working ability. At the same time it is desirable that they should be readily distinguishable and not too alike, or the handler may find himself in further difficulties.

When hunting the dogs together they should always be sent off in opposite directions and encouraged to hunt independently. Any tendency to dog the other's steps, or run jealous, should be promptly checked. At any sign of this the offender should be dropped and sent off in the opposite direction. Occasionally one should be dropped or brought in to heel and the other worked alone, but in that case the same treatment should then be given to the other.

When either dog comes on point the other must be dropped at once if he does not back on sight. The youngster may be taught to back with a reliable steady pointer in the same way as he is taught to point. At the sight of the other stiff and rigid on point it should in any case be instinctive for the dog which is already a staunch pointer to go rigid as well. If a dog shows signs of not backing he should at once be dropped by command, or signal. On no account should he be allowed to steal the other's point, even by accident.

When the game is flushed both dogs should drop at once unless each is on a separate point of his own. If one dog has not observed the flush of game he should in any event drop to shot, unless again he is on a separate point of his own. In general the dog that found the game should be given the retrieve, but in the initial stages of brace work and if there is any sign of kennel jealousy it is important to see that the other dog has the next retrieve if possible. When training two youngsters together it is most important to see that each has his due share of retrieving in this way. If the dogs are on separate points each, if possible, should be dealt with separately.

Even if the handler only has one dog it is always important to teach a youngster to work in harmony with other dogs as part of his more advanced training. If during his training he is introduced to other dogs at every opportunity he should be neither wary nor shy of them. Any tendency to show fight should be thoroughly checked at once, for like constant barking or whining, this is a bad habit which can readily become most objectionable and tiresome. In the earliest stages such bad habits are usually easily enough checked, but once they have had an opportunity to develop they can become an almost ineradicable vice.

When the youngster has reached the stage of training where he is capable of working satisfactorily in conjunction with another dog, and can be relied on not to run in or commit any of the other common crimes, in spite of a bad example being shown him, he can be truly said to be a trained dog. At the same time his general education is not likely to be complete by any means. He may have retrieved rooks and starlings, but not yet woodcock. He may never have seen a grouse, or a goose.

There is likely to be much for the young dog to learn in his first shooting season, and in some cases it may be several seasons before his initial introduction to many aspects of the sport is completed. For instance, the youngster should be introduced to the shooting of duck and pigeon over decoys. He should first be shown the decoys in position with a warning 'Mark No'. A bird may then be thrown near them. If he approaches them he should be rated and sent to retrieve the correct bird. If his training has been properly completed there should be no trouble thereafter. The same thing applies to ferreting. The dog should be introduced to the ferret with the command 'Mark No'. It is to be hoped that thereafter the ferret will be safe. This is all a matter of experience.

It may be argued that these are fine points, but the fact is that the youngster's education has not been completed. Throughout his first season especially he still has a lot to learn. In the first days in the shooting field the handler should always try to think ahead as to the likely effect of his actions on the young dog. The youngster should be given as much experience of different ground and game and types of shooting as possible. The handler will find that it pays considerably to take him out without a gun and merely pick up for friends or work him in front of the guns for others. Apart from anything else, the handler himself will almost certainly learn a lot by doing so.

It is at this stage that the handler may decide to enter his dog in a show, a working test, or a field trial. This is all to the good. At the very least it means that the handler is pleased with his dog. It is to be hoped that the dog will acquit himself well if he has been chosen and trained on the lines indicated. At the same time it is only fair and sensible to give him some preparation first.

As regards shows it is important that the youngster should be trained in what to expect in the show ring and how to comport himself there. He must first be accustomed to crowds. A journey into any large town will probably prove sufficient preparation in this respect. He must also be accustomed to being walked out round the ring at a good pace on the inside of his handler. He must then be accustomed to trotting out in a straight line away from the judge and back again. Then he must be taught to stand well and be accustomed to the judge's handling.

To teach the dog to take the best stance the handler must 'set' the dog in position. Both forelegs should be placed well forward with a lift under the chest. The muzzle may be held up with one hand while the hind legs are adjusted to give the best stance with the other hand, which is then moved, if necessary, to maintain the tail position. Some repetition of this will be necessary before the youngster begins to appreciate what is required. As with any other training, it is advisable not to overdo it, but to accustom the dog to it by degrees.

If necessary an assistant may be used to act as the judge and the entire show routine run through a number of times so that the youngster becomes accustomed to it. This does not mean that a dog which has not been trained in this way stands no chance in the show ring, but he will inevitably be handicapped from the start. Once accustomed to the routine, many dogs become show conscious and deliberately show themselves.

It is advisable for the handler who knows nothing of the subject to go first and see for himself what is required. He will probably do well to start in one of the smaller local shows, where there is less strain on dog and handler. The same advice holds good for working tests and field trials. In practice if the handler has trained his youngster successfully on the lines indicated, he should find that he is likely to perform creditably in either tests or trials. There can be no earthly harm in entering him in any case and it will be good experience for both dog and handler.

Nominations for open stakes, both in working tests and in field trials are often difficult to obtain, even for experienced handlers and their dogs, but in any case the inexperienced handler will no doubt prefer to start in novice tests or trials, however good he may consider his dog. By starting in a small way both handler and dog are likely to acquire confidence. The handler may feel that standardized systems of judging would be desirable, and that on occasions more realism might be introduced, but he will soon realize that there is a considerable element of luck in shows, tests or field trials. He will also no doubt appreciate that the organizers and judges are generally doing the best they can in the circumstances.

Certain people scoff loudly at shows, tests and field trials and talk wildly of the hazards of disease and the strain on the dogs. Others shout loudly about only wanting a 'working dog'. Admittedly a working dog is desirable above everything else, but there is certainly no harm in his being a prize specimen of his breed as well, able to win in the show ring, working tests and field trials. All too often the scoffer has a dog which could never even qualify in either and has little to recommend him beyond his owner's inflated belief in his abilities. It is highly undesirable that there should be any division between various types of dog within the same breeds and these scoffers are doing nothing constructive about the breeds they profess to admire. Let them at least keep their own shortcomings quiet in the same way as those who only support shows, working tests or field trials and do not work their dogs.

It is true that neither shows, working tests nor even field trials are necessarily any criterion of how a dog works with his handler on other occasions or of his worth to his handler. Although it is often forgotten by their more vociferous supporters, they are merely intended as a guide to the serious breeder so that he may aim at producing improved stock. At the same time success in any of these fields will at least be proof that the handler is interested in producing a better-looking gundog which works well and has in part achieved his aims. If he has failed in his first attempt, there is no harm done and another day he may well succeed. It is worth trying.

CHAPTER EIGHT

TESTS AND TRIALS

THERE ARE SEVERAL GOOD REASONS for the average owner entering his, or her, dog in either working tests or novice trials and the principal one, of course, is the desire to see how their dog compares with others. It is a perfectly understandable reaction after the tribulations of training a dog to wish to know how it works in comparison with others. In the normal course of events there are not many chances of making such comparisons during a shooting day and a working test, or novice field trial, may well provide the only opportunity available to do so.

Another common reason for entering working tests, or novice trials, is that the owner has joined a Gundog, or Breed, Society which provides not only training classes, but also working tests at the end of the training session. Increasingly societies are being formed with such aims in mind, usually, although not invariably, approved by the Kennel Club. In that they generally provide the complete novice with an opportunity to see other handlers working their dogs and also act as a useful source of helpful guidance, as well as providing a measure of the progress being made with the young dog, they are a very good thing. For the owner who has no ground suitable for training, or who totally lacks confidence, they can provide very useful, even necessary, help.

Naturally enough, once a dog and owner have been attending a series of training classes and are confident that they are well up to the standards of their class mates, it is only a small step to consider entering a working test where almost all the entrants are known and where any mistakes are likely to be greeted with no more than friendly sympathy. From there it is only another small step to enter a novice trial run by the same society. It is thus that many well known field trial, or working test, competitors, and for that matter judges, have begun.

One of the other quite common reasons for entering tests or novice trials is pure competitiveness and a desire to see one's dog excel. In general people of this kind are extroverts who can accept it, even if not too happily, when they lose. If, however, the competitiveness is deeply ingrained such people can be rather tiresome since it is often the case that they can see no faults in their dog and complain about other competitors, or refuse to accept the judges' decisions, and generally make a thorough and unsporting nuisance of themselves. Everyone who has ever had anything to do with working tests, or trials, will know this type of competitor and generally avoid them as much as possible.

There are also those misguided enthusiasts, who not only can see no faults in their dog but who insist on entering tests, or trials, long before the dog has been sufficiently trained. In a way these unfortunates are the greatest nuisance of all, since it is almost impossible to explain to them that they are spoiling the day for others by using the event as nothing more than a training class, when it is obvious to everyone that their dog stands no chance. Of course, in such cases it is up to the judge to be ruthless and put them out straightaway, but there is always the point that they have paid their entry fee and are entitled to run their dog despite the obvious waste of time involved. It is only after they have been given every chance that such people should be barred from entry, for in the chronic case they will never prove to be more than a tiresome nuisance. Should anyone regard this as an exaggeration they have only to ask an experienced judge of working tests, or trials, or for that matter the hard-working organisers of such events, and they will find it is unfortunately true that these people are by no means uncommon. It is a sad fact that not all dog owners and handlers are level headed and sensible; some of them are also nut-cases and it is generally the case that unbalanced owners have unbalanced dogs.

In general the area required for a working test need not be large. As long as suitably varied terrain is available a mere two or three acres may be sufficient. Ideally, however, something like ten acres with preferably a good viewing point for spectators overlooking the site is desirable. Such an area with water available and some fences, hedgerows, or stone dykes, interspersed to provide obstacles for the competing dogs is ideal. Anyone who has ever attended the Game Fair will have noticed how, almost invariably, excellent ground is chosen for the working gundog competitions and exhibitions, usually with gorse, or small copses, to provide cover and a lake for the water retrieves.

The usual method by which such tests are organised is for each competitor to be asked to perform a succession of tests in turn. These tests are usually graded in difficulty, so that the first is comparatively simple and the last the hardest of all. Thus the first is likely to consist of little more than a straightforward thrown dummy being saluted with a blank cartridge fired in the general direction of the throw. The dog, of course, is judged on each entry for its steadiness, its obedience to its handler's commands and for the speed and style with which it performs the test.

The degree of difficulty involved in the tests should naturally reflect to a large extent the degree of training of the dogs concerned. Advanced working tests may involve

Mr Ian Phillip's F.T. Champion G.S.P. bitch Dunpender Kate, bred by the author and trained on the lines advocated, retrieving a rabbit in a Field Trial.

dummies concealed in cover, or across water, or other obstacles, at a considerable distance from the handler, which have to be retrieved without any shot fired and with the dog working out of sight of the handler, or with other dummies thrown as distractions. Such tests may call for high standards of training and considerable understanding between dog and handler. There is not much doubt that a dog capable of winning in advanced tests of this nature is likely to prove a very useful dog in the shooting field.

Even a simple novice working test requires a good deal of organisation and preparation, which is not always apparent to those competing. For instance when a society decides to hold a working test the committee concerned has to have a meeting to organise the matter. They must first decide on a suitable site, which they know will be available, and choose a date which does not clash with other events. Next they must arrange for a judge, or judges, to be approached with alternative names should their first choices not be available. They must also call for volunteers to help the long-suffering secretary to organise the affair. Apart, perhaps, from deciding on a limit for the number of entrants, the whole affair may then be passed on to the sub-committee with a general sigh of relief.

Given these guidelines the sub-committee thus formed has a comparatively straightforward task. They must first visit the site and decide on the number and variety of tests which can most suitably be arranged within the limitations of the terrain. In a comparatively simple novice test these might consist of first, a dummy thrown into long grass some twenty five yards from the handler with a shot fired, all in full view of the dog and handler so that the fall could be clearly marked. The second test a little further on might then be with the dummy landing beyond an obstacle such as a fence, or ditch, so that the dog has to cross the obstacle both ways to complete the retrieve. The third test might consist of two dummies thrown and a shot being fired with the competitor expected to send his dog for one dummy first, at the judge's discretion, before retrieving the other. The fourth test might be a blind retrieve across an obstacle, possibly working beyond the sight of the handler. Such a series of tests might well make up a very satisfactory novice working test.

It would be desirable for those inspecting the site to calculate how many helpers are likely to be required at each test postion to throw dummies, fire blanks and generally operate each test efficiently. They should then double the number to be on the safe side. They should also try to work out roughly how long each test is likely to take. In this way they can work out approximately how many competitors should be accepted in order to keep the day within set time limits. In practice the time limits are only likely to be dictated by such matters as starting time and daylight hours, always leaving a reasonable break for lunch. It is, however, highly undesirable to have tests still continuing as night descends and this has been known to happen where the organisers have been over-optimistic about the timing or have failed to work out the maximum number of entries they should accept.

The other important points the sub-committee must remember are such details as numbered arm-bands for competitors and arm bands for the judges to distinguish them from the helpers accompanying them. Each helper must also be suitably coached beforehand in his, or her, task on the day and ideally a substitute should be available in case of sickness, or failure to arrive. Dummy launchers, if they are being used, guns and blanks, as well as dummies, if these are not to be provided by competitors, must also be organised in advance.

It will be up to the secretary, with assistance if he can arrange it, to accept the entries, with the correct entry fees, arrange the draw, and then the printing of the programmes. It then only remains to pray for good weather on the day. Given good weather, sufficient entries, good judging, sporting competitors and a good audience, the day may even be a financial success, in which case almost everyone will leave in a glow of euphoria, determined to repeat the performance again the following year. Only the secretary and the members of the sub-committee, plagued with complaints from disgruntled competitors, or trying to find those missing arm-bands, or dummy launchers, may not share the general enthusiasm for a repetition.

While open working tests may require somewhat more varied terrain than simple novice tests they should not require very much more in the way of organisation. Where there is suitable ground available it may even be perfectly feasible to have novice tests in the morning and open tests in the afternoon. The only real difference between the novice and open tests is one of degree. The open tests may include a retrieve over water, another on a laid trail with a simulated break, or one with three dummies rather than merely two and with varied distractions. The unseen retrieves are likely to be of greater severity than in the novice tests and any obstacles to be surmounted more difficult.

Whether the same judge, or judges, will be asked to judge both novice and open tests is a matter for the committee to decide. In general, if only to keep down costs, it is usual to keep the number of judges to a minimum. On the other hand it may well be that for the sake of speed it is desirable that one judge covers possibly the first three tests and another judge the second two, more difficult, tests. It may thus be possible to have two competitors working their dogs in different areas at the same time. As long as there is no danger of one competitor distracting another this may be a perfectly satisfactory arrangement.

In effect an open working test should simulate, as far as possible, the sort of problems which a dog may encounter in the shooting field. Thus an unseen retrieve over an obstacle, or a runner with a zig-zag trail, or a retrieve with another bird falling close-by may all be simulated in these tests. Any dog which can perform well in these conditions should certainly be a useful dog in the shooting field, but working tests should never become an end in themselves. It should always be borne in mind that the aim of working tests is to produce a good working gundog. The aim should not be to produce a gundog which performs well in working tests, although it has to be admitted there are some which are seldom used in any other role. The same is unfortunately true of some gundogs run in field trials, indeed amongst some breeds of gundog this is a well known phenomenon.

The likelihood is that the novice handler who has trained his dog to a good standard and has competed successfully in working tests will decide it is worth his while entering a novice field trial. It is even possible that he may be surprised to find that by comparison with an open working test the novice trial is almost simple. This is not to say that the problems are quite the same, since there is an enormous difference between the difficulties simulated in a working test and those which may be encountered in the reality of even a novice field trail.

The fact of the matter is that however well a working test may be run there is no comparison between a dog retrieving a dummy and a dog retrieving a dead bird, or a runner. It is difficult to estimate softness of mouth when a dog is only retrieving a dummy. With a live, or dead, bird another dimension has to be considered. The dog which is winner of innumerable working tests and has never retrieved a live bird may well baulk at the real thing. Conversely it is not unknown for old experienced gundogs capable of retrieving the wiliest of runners to refuse to look at a dummy, more especially one which has the scent of other dogs on it. When a dog has become accustomed to one method of working, as with humans, it is often difficult to readjust and to change abruptly.

There is also the fact that whereas working tests are mainly concerned with retrieving, even the novice trial may be concerned with other factors such as hunting the ground and pointing, depending on the breed of gundog concerned and the category of trial involved. While working tests may accept more or less any breed of gundog, unless specifically stated otherwise, no gundog may enter field trials other than in the category for the breeds to which it belongs. This limitation means that for most breeds, live game apart, they are not expected to do as much in a novice trial as would be the case in an open working test. On the other hand live game, its scent and the dog's reaction to it, whether hunting, pointing, or retrieving is something that cannot be simulated in the most advanced of tests.

Field Trials, like the gundog breeds themselves, are divided into four groups, one for each grouping of gundogs. There are Retriever trials, for all groups of retrievers recognised in this category, and there are Pointer and setter trials for those groups recognised as either pointers or setters. There are also Spaniel trials for those breeds included under that heading and finally there are H.P.R. trials for German Shorthaired Pointers and those breeds which hunt, point and retrieve. Each type of trial, like each grouping of gundogs, is quite different. Not only are the rules for each type of trial different, but the methods of judging and the principles governing the trials also vary considerably.

The reasons for these variations are basically historical. Prior to the development of the breechloading double-barrelled shotgun and driven shooting in the mid-19th century all gundogs, of whatever breed, had been expected to hunt their ground, find game and retrieve it when shot, whether hunting close like many spaniel and retriever breeds, or further out like setter and pointer breeds and some species of retrievers, or larger spaniels. With the development of driven shooting there came an almost rigid distinction between retrievers and pointers and setters. Spaniels, regarded as utility gundogs, were classified mainly as gamekeepers' dogs.

The first trials held in the 1860s were for pointers and setters, but trials for retrievers soon followed. With the establishment of the Kennel Club in 1873 these two types of field trials were the only ones then recognised. It was not until the turn of the century that after considerable clamour the Spaniel was acknowledged by the Kennel Club as a utility gundog and spaniel trials came to be accepted. Only with the introduction of the German Shorthaired Pointer after the 1939-45 War was it finally accepted by the Kennel Club that a fourth gundog group existed and in the 1970s the H.P.R. trials were accepted. Understandably in the circumstances each type of trial, like each group of gundogs, varies considerably from the others.

The retriever trials are generally organised on the principle that the handlers line up with the guns interspersed between them and the judges each cover the two dogs adjacent to them. In a line of six dogs there would therefore be three judges and preferably at least six, or eight, guns. The dogs are run in the order in which their numbers have been drawn. The line advances with each dog at his handler's heel. When a bird is flushed in front of the line it is shot. The line then stops and the dog next in order for a retrieve is usually sent for it, although the judges may vary this as convenience dictates, depending on the state of the trial and similar factors.

Each dog is marked on the speed and style of its retrieve and the judges decide which dogs are wanted for a second round under another judge. Hard mouth and unsteadiness are eliminating faults, as may be failure to retrieve, or giving tongue, or whining. So the trial continues until the judges are satisfied that they have found the winners on the day. In a novice trial the standards will be lowered and when one bird has been shot the line will halt at once and no others may be shot. Ground game may be ignored. In an open trial with higher standards more than one bird may be shot at once and ground game may also be shot and retrieved. Marking birds shot well down the line may make all the difference between winning and losing, as may a successful retrieve on a runner, especially when another dog has tried and failed to find it.

The setter and pointer trials are run on a very different principle. Here the dogs run together in pairs, according to the numbers they have drawn. Thus each pair of dogs work as a brace, quartering their ground independently, but crossing each other. When one or other dog comes on point the other is expected to honour that point by backing. The judges may then decide to continue until the second dog gets a point, or quite possibly to put only the first dog forward into the second round, depending on how they consider the dogs have both worked. The judges will thus work their way through the dogs in the stake until they have decided which ones they want to have a second run. Those selected are also run in pairs until finally the judges have decided on the winners of the trial, after possibly having had a further run-off. Failure to point, or to back, poor quartering and unsteadiness are eliminating faults.

In novice pointer and setter trials it is customary not to have a gun fired. The game pointed is merely flushed and the dog is expected to honour the flush by dropping, or remaining steady. In open stakes there may be a gun, or pair of guns, and birds may, or may not, be shot. If game is shot a retriever is used for the retrieves. A great deal depends on the owner of the land providing the ground for the trial. Since setter and pointer trials are often held out of season, i.e. in July on grouse, or in February on paired partridges, shooting may, in any event be out of the question. It is not uncommon for setters and pointers to be used solely for trials and never actually to be used in the field for shooting.

Spaniel trials are similar to setter and pointer trials in that the dogs are expected to run in pairs according to the numbers they have drawn. The handlers generally work their dogs between a pair of guns and each dog is expected to work its own ground and to flush game within range of the guns. The dogs may cover in part the ground of the other dog, but it is regarded as a fault if they continually point game instead of flushing it, or if they flush game out of range. Other faults are unsteadiness, failure to honour the flush by dropping, giving tongue and failure to drop on shot. The dog flushing the game is expected to retrieve the bird and is marked accordingly. As with retrievers hard mouth is an eliminating fault. The trial continues in this way until the judges have gone through the list and have decided which dogs they require to run a second time. In this way the winners on the day are finally selected.

The trials for the fourth group of gundogs, namely German Shorthaired Pointers and those breeds which Hunt, Point and Retrieve, known frequently as the H.P.R. breeds, are run rather differently. Only one dog is worked at a time in front of two judges and a line of up to four guns is normally covered by this dog working in front. The dog is expected to quarter the ground, find game and come on point. When the judges are satisfied with the point, the dog is expected to flush the game on command and drop to flush and shot. The dog is then expected to retrieve the game, whether fur or feather, once shot and bring it to hand, whether it has fallen in cover, in, or across, water, or in the open. Finally they are expected to enter water and retrieve from or across water, depending on whether it is a novice or open stake. Either stake is limited to twelve dogs since it has been found that this is as many as two judges working together are likely to be able to judge efficiently in one day. Failure to point, unsteadiness, hard mouth, or failure to enter water are eliminating faults, as may be whining, poor quartering and lack of hunting ability.

Of the four types of trial the latter is probably the most demanding, in that each dog must perform several functions well in front of two judges in order to qualify for a certificate of merit, let alone a place. At the same time, from the field trial organiser's viewpoint, these are amongst the more simple trials to organise since all that is required is suitable ground, which covers virtually any shooting ground, with only enough game for each dog to have a chance of at most two points and two retrieves, as long as there is also water available for the water retrieve. The latter is usually on recently shot pigeons, or game birds when available, thrown into, or across, water, in order to prove that the dogs are able to enter water and retrieve. Only two, or four, guns are required and two judges. With only twelve dogs in the stake the organisation is minimal compared with, for instance, twenty four dogs in a retriever stake.

Perhaps the most important factors for a successful trial are that there should be suitable ground with enough game available. Yet in these respects the requirements for the different groups of gundogs may be very different. Contrary to what might be expected vast numbers of reared game are not required in any field trial, since too much game can be a hindrance rather than a help, making matters difficult for competitors and judges. A reasonable quantity of such game readily available in large fields of roots might, however, be very suitable for a retriever trial, although less desirable for any of the other three groups. In general, for instance, pointer and setter trials require wide open spaces, large fields or moorland, with sufficient ground cover to hold game, but not too much to prevent fast and wide quartering. Spaniels on the other hand are expected to face thick ground cover and young plantations, or grass land with numerous gorse patches, where game birds, hares, or rabbits might take shelter are ideal for them. Theoretically, at least, the H.P.R. breeds should be able to cope with any of these conditions, but ideally a mixture of them all would be most suitable for them. In their case it must also be remembered that an area of water is required for the water retrieve.

As with working tests, once the choice of ground has been made, the most suitable date decided on and a short-list of possible judges made, the organisation of the field trial is generally deputed to a sub-committee and the club secretary.

Unlike Working Tests it is not necessary to consider limiting entries, since in all Trials, excepting those for Pointers and Setters there is an automatic limit on the entries which can be accepted. Even so it is advisable to ensure a prompt and early start to the Trial so that darkness does not fall before the winner has been chosen, which is something that can all too easily happen in short winter days. It is also highly desirable to ensure that the owner of the ground and host, or hostess, for the day is not given any possible reason to object to the behaviour of anyone present, whether competitor, spectator or even judge. Although not necessarily directly involved, he, or she, is the one person whom the club cannot afford to offend if they wish to be invited to use that ground again and good ground for field trials is not easily found.

Generally the headkeeper, but sometimes the landowner himself, or herself, will act as Steward of the Beat, suggesting which ground to take, in consultation with the judges as to their requirements.

In some cases the judges may favour starting on ground with not much game and ending on ground with rather more to ensure a successful day, but in other cases the exact reverse might be true, since much has to depend on the type of Trial and gundog group. In any event such questions as wind, scenting conditions, ground cover and the type of terrain will have to be discussed as well as the likely amount of game to be encountered. In addition the guns will have to be briefed on the requirements of the trial, which, of course, varies not only with each gundog group, but also according to whether it is a novice or open stake.

Much has to depend on the circumstances of the day and it is important that the field trial organiser, the landowner, or the headkeeper, and the judges should all work together as a team. Basically it is up to the organiser to ensure that this happens. He has to function as a middle-man, anticipating the judges' requirements, checking with them and the landowner, or headkeeper, prior to the start and at intervals throughout the day. Although, with experienced judges, it is unlikely that they will make any mistakes, it is up to the organiser to ensure that this does not occur, that each competitor is available when required and, in short, that the day runs smoothly.

The organiser himself will either stay in the line with the judges, or a little way behind, accompanied by a Steward, or assistant, to act as runner to pass back any messages to competitors and spectators behind the red flag. He must see that the next competitors, who may be required are always ready and waiting to take their places in the line. It is also up to the organiser, after consultation with the judges and headkeeper, or landowner, to decide on when to stop for lunch. Then he has to arrange suitable refreshment for the judges and others whom he feels may merit it.

An experienced landowner, or headkeeper, who understands what is required, working in conjunction with an experienced senior judge, can be of enormous assistance. In those circumstances the organiser can heave a sigh of relief and cease to worry about that side of affairs. Experienced judges will also ensure that there are few complaints from competitors. They will recognise at a glance the old hand working next to a young and inexperienced novice, who is trying to use his greater experience to his advantage by casting his dog over the other's ground, by using whistles calculated to mislead the other dog, or by any of the numerous ways open to competitors, which may be regarded as gamesmanship rather than as cheating. Such old tricks as getting between the dog and game to be flushed, prodding on a sticky pointer, deliberately wringing the neck of a bird already dead to give the impression of soft mouth, when in fact the dog has 'closed the suitcase', will not deceive an experienced eye. Apart from not being deceived by such dodges, a good judge will always look for the best in each competitor, marking up, rather than merely looking for faults and taking every opportunity to mark them down, which is a method all too often used, though seldom with satisfactory results. With able judges there is little time wasted and in this respect also the organiser's task is made easier.

It is up to the organiser to arrange beforehand, through the headkeeper if necessary, for helpers to be ready to carry the game shot, also for a reliable person to be on hand to carry a red flag behind which the spectators and competitors waiting their turn to run must stand. It is important that the red flag bearer not only knows the ground, but also has a sound knowledge of both shooting and gundogs so that he can keep a suitable distance from events, striking a happy mean between safety, visibility and interference. Nothing is more annoying for judges, or competitors, than hearing a steady buzz of conversation close behind them, alarming game and distracting the dog's attention. It is also most disconcerting for guns to swing round on a bird and find stray spectators wandering in the line of fire. It is essential that they stay with the red flag bearer and that he keeps them under control, neither too close, nor too far, from the proceedings.

When the last competitor has had his run and the judges are deciding on the winners, the organiser has to ensure that the armbands are all returned, that the various game-carriers, stewards, red flag bearers and other helpers, as well as the headkeeper himself, are suitably rewarded, refreshed and thanked. He must have the prizes, including perpetual trophies, ready on hand for the awards when they are made, with a suitable person such as the host's wife persuaded to present them. He must see that the judges are also suitably refreshed and thanked for their efforts, as well as prompting them to send him their report on the day as soon as possible, so that it can be distributed to the local and sporting press for publication. Finally, he has to deal with any complaints, whether from irritated spectators, who failed to see as much as they had hoped, from disgruntled competitors, who could not understand the judges' decisions, or from any other source.

It is not altogether surprising that the ideal field trial secretary or organiser, is hard to find. Few people appreciate the amount of work which is required behind the scenes, although most people are only too ready to blame them when anything goes wrong. On the other hand not many people are ready to give much useful assistance and altogether there are few satisfactions to be gained. Not only is the amount of paperwork considerable, but there is also a great deal of telephoning involved. Inevitably, however meticulously the expenses are recorded, the out-of-pocket expenses and honorariums provided by most Clubs barely cover anything like the amounts expended.

This is one of those demanding positions which requires tact of a high order and acceptance of many extra burdens uncomplainingly. Altogether it is scarcely surprising that there are not many of this dedicated breed to be found. It is up to all field trial competitors to do their best to ease their burden for there is always the danger that one day they might find themselves in this unenviable position. If that ever happens they will at least have the satisfaction of knowing that when they have completed their stint they may not know much more about gundogs, but there will be little more they either wish, or need, to know about field trials.

CHAPTER NINE

CARE AND MANAGEMENT

THERE ARE ALWAYS POINTS which even gundog owners of long standing can learn about the care and management of their dogs. I am frequently appalled by the careless way in which so-called sportsmen sometimes treat their animals. It used to be a sound cavalry motto that horses came first, weapons next and men last when the day was over. Too often one sees dogs merely ordered into the back of a car while the owner goes on to gossip after a shoot.

It cannot be too strongly emphasized that the dog who has worked well for his master during a hard day's sport deserves well of him at the finish. It is worth making a point of always carrying a towel or piece of sacking, or even a copy of *The Times*, so that a wet dog may be dried and comfortably bedded down on an old rug or straw bed before his master sits down to discuss the day. A quick inspection of the dog's pads and body should be made for cuts, barbed wire gashes and thorns. If the dog wants a drink of water, that should be provided, and a reward in the shape of a small feed might not come amiss. Such small attentions do not take long and they go a long way towards lengthening the dog's working life by staving off crippling attacks of rheumatism or arthritis, or other ills.

It is not a good idea incidentally to make the dog travel in the boot of a car or the rear of an estate wagon with the back doors open. Exhaust fumes can be very readily sucked into the boot or the back of an estate wagon in these circumstances, and even if they do not asphyxiate the dog they are likely to render him deaf. This is also a point to appreciate if there is a leak in the exhaust of a car. Fumes which may not be particularly noticeable to humans may have a very damaging effect on a dog.

While it may seem elementary, it should be stressed that feeding a dog during a shooting lunch should always be avoided. If a cheese or garlic sandwich is fed to a dog the handler need scarcely be surprised if his nose is affected. Far worse, of course, is the careless feeding of chicken or game bones. Although I thought almost everyone knew that such bones can fracture in the dog's intestines and pierce the gut, I have seen them tossed to a dog at a shooting lunch, or alternatively thrown carelessly away where a dog could readily find them. I have also personally known two dogs killed in this way.

It is worth therefore, at the risk of appearing once again to stress the obvious, to start at the beginning. It has already been described how the pup should be dealt with on arrival. He should certainly be made much of, but when the time comes for him to be bedded down for the night give him a mild sedative such as a crushed tablet of aspirin in some warm milk, then give him a run, then introduce him to his bed. If the straw or blanket has been rubbed round his body he should accept the body scent readily enough, and is likely to settle down comparatively quickly. On no account, however, should he be allowed to win that first round.

If the pup is to live in the house, he should have his own private corner with his water bowl and basket to which he can retire. It should hardly need to be pointed out that this should be raised well clear of the ground and draughts. I have seen owners, who should have known better, expect their dogs to bed down each night on a stone floor with only an old rug between them and the stone. In such circumstances it is scarcely surprising that the dogs developed rheumatics at an early age and had their working life consequently unnecessarily shortened. Any cold or damp bed will inevitably result at the least in the dog getting little real rest and more probably developing needless ailments which could quite possibly lead to his premature death.

As well as having a comfortable and draught-free bed the dog should have a regular routine. It is as well to remember that routine in training is also a good thing when it is extended to everyday living for a gundog. A run first thing in the morning. A brush all over with a stiffish brush and if a collar is worn with a name tab on it put the collar on at once. At various periods in the day the dog may expect his routine outings and lessons, or possibly work. In the early evening he has his meal. Immediately afterwards he has another run. Last thing before he beds down for the day after a final outing his collar is removed.

To begin with it may be inadvisable to use a collar and preferable to run the pup in harness. This prevents choking, pulling, and out-at-elbows action developing in a pup with that tendency. Later on when working, especially in cover, a collar can be a considerable handicap to a dog and possibly even a source of danger. It is therefore advisable to run the dog when at work in a slip lead. This simply slips over the dog's head and is adjustable.

If the dog is sleeping in the house on blankets, it is as well that they should be shaken out and brushed each day, as apart from possible dirt they will almost certainly be covered with hairs. While it does not do to disinfect everything too thoroughly, there is no need for the smell of dog to become offensive. Anyone who keeps a dog in the house must be prepared to accept some small side effects. It is hopeless, for instance, being too houseproud about muddy foot marks in wet weather. If the dog is expected to dry his feet himself he would certainly prefer to live in a kennel. Like bachelors, most dogs have a horror of women running after them cleaning up all the time.

If the dog is to live out, advice on kennelling must be somewhat general, since everyone will be guided chiefly by their own special circumstances. All that can really be said is that it should be sound (i.e. dry and draught-proof), secure (i.e. well fenced), as well as clean and comfortable. From a dog's viewpoint comfort merely implies a warm bed. A fair-sized box allowing the dog room to stand, turn and lie at full length, raised off the ground in a garage of ordinary size with an outside run would be a very good makeshift.

Bedding may consist of straw, preferably wheat, which should be changed daily, or a canvas mattress stuffed with straw. Oat and barley straw are not as good as wheat straw, being much more liable to irritate a dog's skin. Sawdust or wood shavings are bad, since they are indigestible, if eaten, as they almost certainly will be. Whatever bedding is used should be clean and free from dust or dirt. Apart from the bedding being changed daily, the kennels themselves should be disinfected at intervals and thoroughly cleaned out.

Fencing should be strong and sufficiently high to prevent the dog leaping out, or, in the case of a bitch, another dog leaping in. It may even be advisable in some cases to cover the run as well. The fencing should be sunk into the ground and stones or concrete added to prevent burrowing out. Sufficient run should be made to avoid the appearance of a cage and to give the dog room to exercise. Old chicken runs and ordinary wire netting simply will not do, as the average dog can chew through it at will, and this sort of makeshift is asking for trouble.

Concrete in the run is easy to clean, but hard on the dog's feet. If it is used, a raised wooden board for the dog to lie on should be added. A shelter from undue sun or wind should also be provided to give shade and protection. Probably grass or earth in the run is best if it can be arranged, but to avoid disease due to stale urine it may need to be dug over from time to time and fresh earth added. Some people advocate cinders, but in a small kennel I can see no advantage in them.

I am against any form of heating in the kennels, as to my mind this is destroying one of the whole objects of keeping a gundog in kennels in the first place. That, of course, must be qualified as being intended with regard to gundogs kept in this country only. Air conditioning or heating may well be essential in some climates. In this country the points already discussed should be sufficient.

In the case of a dog which is kept half in the house and half in the kennel, or with puppies, or whelping bitches, heating may at times, however, be desirable during a really cold spell. In that case, needless to say, great care must be taken that there can be no danger of fire. Exposed cables, terminals or switches within the dog's reach, or any possibility of a heater being upset and coming in contact with inflammable bedding, must at all costs be avoided.

With regard to feeding, it is important that the dog should always have a fresh supply of water available, but, apart from the needs of a pup or a whelping bitch, feeding should be restricted to one meal a day. Once again it is desirable to remember that a gundog is a working dog. To feed first thing in the morning or in the middle of the day is to mean that when working the routine is either going to be broken and the dog will be ravenous by the end of the day, or else the dog will be expected to work on a full stomach, which cannot but make him sluggish and is clearly not good for him. On all counts it is preferable to feed the dog once only in the evening.

Feeding is always a problem which can cause more arguments than almost anything else connected with dogs. Nutrition with human beings is a similar fruitful cause of argument. In fact, there is little doubt that in nature the dog is a meat-eating animal and raw meat in reasonable quantities is undoubtedly a sound diet. That is not to say that an unvaried meat diet is necessarily a good thing. Milk occasionally, fish and vegetables now and then, and good sound wholemeal biscuit or hound-meal to make up a balanced diet is a sound basis to work on.

Almost any food fed to excess is a mistake. Porridge, is what many Scots collies have lived on throughout their working life and it is a sound standby. It can, however, cause skin and teeth troubles, and the same may be said against almost any similar unbalanced unvaried diet. Occasional greens, or roughage, are a necessity. A dog will be seen occasionally, as will cats, almost grazing on grass, but this is purely as an emetic. The dog knows that it requires a clean out and this is Nature's way of doing it.

Bones are another subject on which there are several views. Many people will argue that their dogs have never had bones and are none the worse for it. Others will say that their dogs have always had bones at regular intervals. My own view is that some dogs like and need a bone occasionally and others seldom want them and this is true of most foods. Although a good doer will thrive on almost any food, there is no doubt that some dogs thrive on one thing and some on another. It is worth remembering that fish will generally tempt a faddy feeder and this extends to oily fish such as sardines. Dogs, like humans, have their likes and dislikes, and it is as well to study them.

Anyone who has ever handled a number of animals will very quickly appreciate the truth of the statement that they all have different ways and different tastes. This is especially noticeable at feeding-time. Some dogs will gobble their food and others are finicky eaters. Some dogs will eat anything put in front of them and others even when almost starving will turn up their noses, or at least look twice at some foods. Some dogs are inveterate scavengers however well fed and others are not. It is a question always of studying the dog and finding out what he thrives on best and in what quantities.

It is as well to remember that with the climate the dog's appetite may wax or wane. Similarly a dog working hard needs more than a dog getting very little exercise. It is absurd to feed each day the same amount without taking this point into account, but many people do forget this and simply feed the same rather unimaginative meals to their dog every day whether working or not. The dog's food should be matched to the work he is doing if he is to be kept fit.

Perhaps it should be noted that white bread contains agene which has been proved to cause fits in dogs and therefore should never be fed to them. Similarly it is perhaps as well to consider whether your dog will necessarily enjoy all the left-overs from the various meals you have been having. Dogs do not do well on custard puddings, spaghetti and garlic and similar dishes. A good dog deserves to be well fed.

The dog's appetite should generally be a reliable guide to how he is feeling. When he is off his food it is as well to watch for other symptoms. A dull eye, dry nose, staring coat, and general listlessness probably indicates a temperature. Ribs prominent, stomach tucked up, excessive appetite or thirst are other danger signs to look for, and if it is felt advisable it may be as well to visit the vet. There is never any excuse for failing to notice or ignoring symptoms of illness.

If the handler decides on a bitch pup as easier to train, he will have to bear in mind that twice a year he is going to have her coming into season. The first occasion is usually about 6–9 months although this may be missed altogether. Thereafter he should keep a record expecting the heats at about six months intervals. He should keep his eyes open for any swelling of the glands and also watch the bitch's behaviour. As soon as he is reasonably sure he sees signs of approaching season he should begin to take care.

The handler's first step should be to apply an easily bought formula to disguise the mating smell. He should also feed pills to the bitch which will help to disguise the smell. It is possible by heavily dosing the bitch in this way to keep her fairly clear of dog approaches. It is, however, essential that she does not get free on her own at this time and that no dog can break into her kennel if she is confined outside. If necessary, when the owner does not feel confident of his own arrangements, it might be as well to send her to a kennels for the period of her heat.

Sooner or later the owner of a bitch will probably feel he wants to breed from her, but his first step in this case should be to take some sound advice from experienced breeders. He should, of course, have bought a bitch which is registered at the Kennel Club in the first place. He should now, if he decides to breed, choose a K.C. registered sire. It is not necessarily always desirable to take the sire with the most impressive list of K.C. show and field trial awards. For various reasons, such as their owners being too busy, or not interested, many good dogs are not entered for shows or trials. As long as the owner feels he likes the dog well enough, as long as it works well, moves well, is representative of the breed, and is not too closely related to his bitch, he may do worse than use it as a sire, but if he is doubtful on any of these points he should certainly seek advice.

Neither dog nor bitch should be too fat. Both should be fit and in good condition. It is desirable to take the bitch to the dog on the eleventh day of colour showing in the bitch. Between then and the thirteenth day it may be possible to get two matings with an interval of a day between them. This should ensure that the bitch is in whelp. It is advisable with a maiden bitch to take her on a lead. Allow the dog and bitch a few moments together free to get to know each other and then slip the lead on again while the dog serves her. Otherwise there is a possible danger of the bitch pulling away and damaging the dog physically.

Lack of any interest on the dog's part or a disinclination on her part to have anything to do with him may almost certainly be put down to incorrect timing. The usual fault most people commit is in trying to get their bitch served too soon, before the right time. The same symptoms, of course, take place if it is overdue also, so that correct timing is an important point to watch.

The essential thing about a whelping bitch (and it is astounding how many otherwise sensible people seem to overlook the point) is that she should be fed an extremely nutritious diet strong in vitamins, especially calcium. Eggs and milk are a sound basis, but good meat and a certain amount of yeast pills are a useful part of the diet. She should also have steady exercise, but should not in the latter stages of her pregnancy be allowed to jump unduly or strain herself in similar ways. Clearly long swims in cold water or undue exposure of any kind are not good for her or her pups. This sort of thing can easily cause mastitis or milk fever.

The bitch will have a gestation period of approximately sixty-three days. In the first instance she will almost certainly whelp some time during the night. It is advisable to prepare a whelping box for her, where she will have privacy and plenty of room to stand up and move around. She should be introduced to this in plenty of time and allowed to make her own bed in it. She will usually tear up the bedding and arrange it in the form of a nest around her. This is to be expected, but underneath should be a roughish sacking floor or carpeting which allows the pups' feet something to push against in order to get at their mother's teats.

The bitch can probably manage the whole business by herself, but most owners will prefer to stand by her in case she has any difficulties. She will probably start at night and there should not be intervals of much more than an hour between pups. If the intervals extend to much more than three hours, it may well be advisable to call the vet, as there may be trouble in the form of a reversed pup or a stoppage of some sort.

As she whelps it is advisable to remove the pups, remove the enveloping membranes, and cut the umbilical cord some 3 or 4 inches from the pup's belly. If the bitch is busy eating the afterbirth, leave her to it, and set about drying the pup vigorously in a piece of rough towelling. It should then be placed on a covered hot-water bottle in a warm box with the other pups, or else given to the mother to lick for a little. She should be left with one pup, but it is advisable to watch that in her uneasy struggles while having the other pups she does not lie on it. If there is any danger of this, it should be rescued and placed with the others.

Some bitches are very easily disturbed about the whole business and become excited while the pups are arriving. Others take it as a matter of course and are grateful for their owner's help and presence. An excitable bitch is one to watch, as she may chew the umbilical cords too close and rupture the pups. There is even a danger if the bitch has been inadequately fed that she may turn cannibal and eat her pups. An extremely nervous or excitable bitch might also damage her pups by accident. Moving round the box in any case is inevitable and therefore on all counts it is preferable to move the pups in case they are accidentally overlaid.

Once the entire litter has been born it is only necessary to see that they can all suck. A strong pup will soon get the hang of this without much teaching. This is the time to examine the whole litter carefully and any deformed or obviously poorly developed pups should be disposed of at once. There is clearly no point in keeping them if they are going to be of no use. It is, in fact, a mistaken kindness to do so.

Immediately after the whelping the bitch should be offered a warm meal of meat broth and slops, or something similar. Warm milk may do no harm. Possibly a little mild laxative may be desirable, but this is largely a question of watching how she behaves. She may be reluctant to leave her pups, but she should be made to do so at reasonably regular intervals.

It should scarcely be necessary to add that she should always have water available, and that for the whole of the time she is nursing the pups she should be extremely well fed. During this period she should be fed four meals or so a day. For as long as she is nursing the pups and feeding them she is earning all she can eat. After four weeks or so she will probably start to regurgitate food to her pups. It is important therefore that she should have good lean meat and not fats and that her food should all be nutritious, not mere bulk feeding. Almost as much as during pregnancy the way the bitch is fed now will affect the pups' start in life. It is false economy to stint her at any stage if it is desired to breed sound pups.

Inevitably, however, the pups will get round worms. This is unavoidable, but it can retard the pups' growth, and if not attended to can even kill them. The pups will require worming at about six weeks, and when they are finally weaned they will probably require it again. This can be simply accomplished with modern tablets, and the pup should soon show signs of picking up again afterwards.

From the time the pups are weaned they should also be receiving four meals a day. Starting with a milk and egg meal in the morning, they should go on to two meals of meat and biscuits during the day and end with another milk meal in the evening. It is an extremely short-sighted policy to skimp the pups or to make up the bulk of their meals with non-nutritious diets of bulk foods. Now is the time when they will prepare for so much future growth and now is the moment when they can be severely set back possibly for life. If they get a good start pups will grow into better dogs and it should be the aim of every breeder to produce the best dogs he can.

The same point should be borne in mind when a pup is selected from a litter. It needs feeding up and care then more than at any other period in its life, except perhaps when an expectant or nursing mother. Anything other than this treatment at these times is tantamount to stupidity and extremely shortsighted. Eggs and milk and other high-protein foods should be provided in plenty.

If pups are to have their tails docked or dew claws

removed, it is advisable to do this on the second or third days. They will feel it less then and will soon recover from the setback, whereas at a later date it is liable to be much more painful and may need an anaesthetic. Dew claws should always be removed, since if they are left on they may be torn out when the dog is exercising as an adult and can then cause a very painful injury. It so happens, too, that if the dog has a cut or other tear on the face and the dew claws have been left on, it is liable to be greatly aggravated due to the dog scratching at it and catching it with his dew claw. They serve no good purpose and are better removed.

It should be mentioned that injections are now available against hard pad and distemper which can be given at six weeks. It is well worth the small expense involved to have this done. Later it is advisable to have routine injections against the other common dog scourges such as lepto-spirosis. Anyone who has seen any of these diseases would never hesitate or delay for an instant. It should also be added that in the case of a pup especially any signs of listlessness or lack of appetite should be watched very carefully. If it is felt necessary the pup should be taken to the vet without delay. If he has not been fully immunized, it is as well to remember that infected dogs may have been visiting the vet; therefore it is better to carry the pup and avoid any risk of infection.

Having thus dealt very briefly with the main points concerning the care and management of gundogs, it may be as well to mention the subject of adult vices. Strictly speaking, this is a question of training, but it is usually caused by lack of care and good management. A dog becomes bored because his kennel routine is badly arranged, or he has too small a run, or insufficient exercise. The result is the same. To relieve the monotony, to work off excess spirits, or simply because he is fed up, the dog develops some vice which, if not checked at once, may readily become incorrigible.

This may simply take the form of barking loudly and continuously. It may take the form of digging persistently in the kennel run, or of deliberately chewing the kennel fittings and destroying them. Holes in the kennel run may be filled with earth soaked in creosote. Timber may be creosoted or covered with metal to stop chewing. Barking may be checked at every opportunity. This, however, is treating the symptoms not the root cause. The dog may need company, a new routine, a new diet. Look always for the cause and cure it if possible at the first sign of trouble.

More serious is the dog which develops a propensity for chasing sheep or killing poultry. If the dog is not properly kennelled or exercised and is allowed to roam at will without sufficient work, and if there are sheep or poultry in the vicinity, he can scarcely be blamed for chasing them when they run. The blame is clearly the owner's for his lack of care. Correct kennel management and routine should never allow such a vice to develop. Correctly trained the pup should have early been introduced to both sheep and poultry with the prohibition 'No'. Once such a situation has arisen and before it has become an ingrained vice a cure may be possible.

An old cure used to be tying the dead bird or beast round the dog's neck so that it remained there for several days. A more humane and less messy method of dealing with a sheep chaser, which I can vouch for personally, is putting the dog in a pen with an old black-faced ewe and her lamb. After he has been repeatedly butted with her horns he will be glad to escape when he is allowed out. Thereafter he is unlikely to look at a sheep again.

An electronic collar can be useful here. This device is

simply a 'shocking box' fitted to a collar strapped tightly round the dog's neck. By means of an electronic circuit a shock can be transmitted to the dog at a distance of a quarter of a mile. He is allowed to range free and the moment he shows any interest in either sheep or poultry he is subjected to an electronic shock at long range. I am told that quick and permanent cures have been effected in this way.

It is not advisable for the amateur trainer, however, to rush off at once to buy an electronic collar. To start with they are very expensive. Disregarding that point, it is doubtful whether they should be recommended for anyone who is not experienced in training. Certainly their use on anything but a mature dog would be likely to cause trouble. Used on a mature dog to correct vice or ingrained faults the device should be very useful in experienced hands, but obviously, like the check cord, a dog is liable to become accustomed to it if it is used too much and will work perfectly with it on, but not otherwise.

It is to be hoped the need for such devices will not arise. If the dog is properly kennelled and exercised regularly, he will not have the opportunity or the desire to go off self-hunting and develop other vices. Taken with care through the stages of training described, the average dog and the average handler should be able to attain a degree of mutual understanding and mutual competence which will make their work in the shooting field a pleasure to them both. Although both should enjoy the training, the handler should never forget that the ultimate aim is their maximum efficiency as a team together when they are out with the gun. He will soon realize that to achieve this there is always something fresh to learn.

INDEX